The Secret Lives of Men

The Secret Lives of Men

~

A Collection of My Homoerotic Stories

By
Nicolas Mann

Nicolas Mann
Enterprises

Printed in the United States.

Cover Design by Matt Helm
Photograph by Nicolas Mann
Text Design by Nicolas Mann
Thanks to James Westerland
Final Editing by Vivian Fox

ISBN 978-0-578-01335-0

For Matthew, my partner, my love, my buddy, you mean so much to me.

For Kib, who wasted so much time with me, I love you.

For Darrel and Daniel, thank you guys.

♂

TABLE OF CONTENTS

·Introduction x

Night Duty.. 1

To Protect and Serve 15

Summer of Love..26

Mr. Tucker...41

Lost Daddy 50

Bar Tale...62

Mountain Men..69

The Manhandler Saloon 98

Newt's First Lesson....................................109

Guy's New Toys..119

An Extra Pair 134

Bless Me Father 148

The Ghost of Dark Oak Cottage.................157

About The Author.......................................181

·INTRODUCTION

I am Nicolas, Nick to my friends and Nicky to my family and those that know me best. It's a boyish – girly name I know, but one that means they feel especially close to me and I like that.

Through my 50 some odd years I've known many people. They have traveled through my life like leaves in the wind on their way to what they feel is their destiny. They come and go, some linger for awhile or leave so suddenly that I think maybe they were merely specters, so they are like dreams. Some I still recall, some I can't remember, and some I'll never forget.

I've found and lost love and thought my heart would never mend. I've been trusted, been mistreated and forsaken. I've been passionately kissed, routinely slapped, spat at and mugged, left for dead and betrayed. I've been in bar room brawls and back room orgies. I've been congratulated, scolded, and reprimanded. My life has been good and bad, full and strange and I've cried and thought that life couldn't be any worse.

I've met the great, near great, and soon to be great. I've rubbed elbows with mayors and governors – from the fancy to the not so fancy. I've stayed in abandoned houses on forgotten sides of town and mansions on the rocky shores of the pacific. I've wished, wanted, and stolen. I've prayed to God and wondered if there was anyone really there to listen, I've sinned and repented only to sin again. I am like so many that scarcely anything sets me apart.

Then I sit and start to write and decide that I am not like anyone else. Sometimes the ideas come and sometimes they don't but again they are like dreams. I see them in my head. The characters and their words, they speak, not to me but to each other and I write down what they say. I'm just the court appointed stenographer.

I'm not a very good speaker, I mumble, get nervous and start to stutter and stammer so I write to make myself clear.

Sometimes the words don't come easy so I have to listen hard.

What follows are the stories dreamy characters tell – enjoy.

~

Night Duty

Lanny stood in the service elevator, idly massaging his unshaven jaw, sore from a brawl the night before. He was on his way up to the Anthropology Department, mop and pail in hand. The old lift hummed curiously. Every few seconds it groaned and the compartment trembled.

"Come on ol' boy," he whispered, "stay with me." After some long minutes, it bounced to halt on the third floor. He straightened the frayed collar of his old gray coveralls and brushed away imaginary dirt as he waited for the bent and bruised doors to open.

"Damn," he grumbled after looking down. "Shoulda' wore underwear." There was no mistaking the obvious bulge at his crotch. He wanted to make a good impression, but not like this. These intellectual types intimidated him as it was, and he didn't want to appear like an uneducated red-neck, so he adjusted himself, trying without much success to mask his manhood. He glanced at his watch; it was just past midnight.

The hall was dark, quiet, and a faint, stale odor hung heavily in the air. His footsteps echoed as he made his way past the sleeping offices. At the far end, a stream of amber light spilled across the dark floor, its warming glow inviting him into the Anthropology Department.

Just outside, he paused for a moment then knocked and peered in.

"Maintenance!" he said loudly. "Hello?"

"Yeah, back here," said a deep, disembodied voice. Lanny set his gear down and walked to the back office. The room was lit by a solitary green glass desk lamp, barely illuminating a shaggy-haired man looking rather large and imposing, sitting behind a wide desk. The eerie light reflected off his round glasses, giving them an unnatural glow. In front of him were stacks of books and manuscripts.

"Y'all called for someone?" Lanny asked, his voice betraying the twang of an Arkansas accent. The man wrinkled his brow and looked at his watch.

"That was two hours ago." He protested.

"I'm sorry sir. My shift just started, and I came as soon as I saw the message.

"Yeah, well it's too late now." The man growled. "I had to clean up the friggin' mess myself."

"Well, big whoopty doo," Lanny thought.

"I'm sorry sir, is there anythin' else I can help ya with?" The man didn't speak, nor did he get up.

"Sir?" Lanny repeated.

"Well actually, yes," he finally said. "Could you hand me that briefcase?"

Lanny looked around, at first not seeing it then noticed it was only a few feet away from the seated man.

"Well shit!" Lanny thought *"Why can't he get up off his fat ass and get it himself?"* The man was clearly making him grovel.

"That'n right jer?" Lanny pointed.

"Yes, please, bring it here."

"Damn!" he thought.

Lanny was annoyed but for the sake of argument, did what was asked. Angrily, he snatched up the briefcase, walked around and held it out before the man; who still remained sitting. All at once Lanny drew in his breath and stepped back a few paces, noticing the poor man couldn't possibly get up; he was in a wheelchair.

"Oh shit, I'm sorry," Lanny blurted out. The man lowered his glasses and looked up.

"Scuze me?" he asked.

"I…I didn't know." Lanny stuttered.

"What this?" The man asked patting the handrails. "I figured everyone knew." He added and took the briefcase.

"You're new here aren't you?"

"Yes sir, I started about three weeks ago. I'm really sorry, I didn't realize."

"Well that's ok. I've been in this so many years that I sometimes forget," he said while scanning the janitor and his shabby attire. Lanny stood a moment not knowing what to do or what further to say.

"Um, well I better git back to m' duties," he said then started to walk away. The professor wheeled himself around the desk and was rolling toward Lanny.

"I should introduce myself," he said reaching out his hand. "My name's Owen. I'm the Professor Hardaway advertised on the door." Lanny looked to the door then to the man's hand. Without thinking, he wiped his hand on his coveralls before returning the gesture.

"Pleased to meet cha'," he said. "I'm Lanny, the night janitor." The professor accepted his hand, shook, but held on a little too long for Lanny's comfort.

"Oh, sorry." Lanny pulled back. As if he had insulted the man.

"Don't apologize; I was just noticing how physically powerful your hand was. As it says on the door; I'm an

Anthropologist, and it is the study of man," he said. "I have a bad habit of studying…men." He added.

The professor's grip was strong too, Lanny noticed. His shoulders were broad like a linebacker's, while his arms and chest were like those of a weight-lifter. But his face was quietly handsome, perfectly framed by his unkempt hair and salt and pepper colored beard. Under bushy eye brows, his piercing blue eyes scanned Lanny's lean, muscular body with keen interest before settling on the custodian's noticeable bulge. They said nothing for a few uncomfortable seconds, but Lanny felt the usual twinge brought on by the professor's open stare.

"Well, I best be goin'," he said again. At the door he turned around, "Give me a holler if'n y'all need anythin'." The professor nodded and watched Lanny pick up his tools then disappear into the men's room across the hall.

Once inside, Lanny was finally able to relax.

"Damn!" he said out loud. He thought about the professor staring at his crotch and subconsciously groped himself. Sometimes, the mere look from a man excited him. Hard cock aside, it was back to work; he made a quick examination of the sink and mirrors. The walls and floor were made of inexpensive marble, even the stall partitions were marble. Over the urinal were hand scribed messages offering sexual favors with long past dates. One read: blow jobs in last stall. Out of curiosity, Lanny went to the stall and found the walls scrawled with crudely drawn pictures and surprisingly, a glory hole. He fondled himself again while wondering how long it had taken someone to gouge out the marble, then checked the other stall. There were more drawings and some were actually quite good. His mop and pail forgotten, he got more excited. He stepped in, undid the buttons of his coveralls, and sat down.

He spread his legs as he reached up under his t-shirt and tweaked his hardening nipples. Beside the hole was an elaborate drawing of a cock spewing cum, someone had taken great care to draw this one; it was richly detailed with veins running along the thick shaft and drippy cum oozing out the piss slit. It was funny he thought, even here in these hallowed halls, educated men couldn't resist the lustful need of wanting head or reveling in the joys of sucking another man's cock. Lanny seemed unusually horny now, and his cock was fully hard, so he wasted no time in giving it attention.

Eyes closed; Lanny idled in his one handed massage when suddenly the boom of the men's room door being forcefully pushed opened made him bolt upright. Startled, he cocked his head to one side and listened. He heard the sound of rubber wheels squeaking across the marble floor, stop for a moment, then continue on to the other stall.

After some initial maneuvering and fumbling, the new comer was seated. Lanny sat quietly resisting the temptation to look, but soon curiosity overcame him and cautiously, he lowered his face to the opening.

Professor Owen Hardaway was seated looking forward. Lanny studied the older man and noticed his thighs; they were a little thin, but covered with dark hair. Suddenly, the professor turned and caught Lanny's gaze. Quickly, Lanny jerked back.

"*Damn!*" he thought. Lanny tried to come up with something clever to say, when he heard a familiar sound. He looked again; the professor had leaned back and opened his shirt. His eyes were closed, head bent back and one hand pinched his nipple. His whole upper body was incredibly muscled under a rich pelt of white and black hair. Further down his body, resting between his hairy thighs was a thick, vein-ribbed cock. Lanny watched as the professor reached down and sensuously slid the ample skin back, exposing a head glistening with pre-cum, then turned towards Lanny and winked.

"Like it?" the professor asked devilishly. His deep voice rumbled, piercing the hollow-quiet of the men's room. Then he leaned forward and whispered, "Let's see what you got in them coveralls, boy!" The man's sensuous voice sent a chill through him. Lanny stood up letting his coveralls fall, arrogantly exposing himself.

"Oh yeah," the professor hissed. "Bring it here!" Lanny moved forward, inserting his impressive cock into the hole. It was only a second before he felt the warm wetness of Professor Owen Hardaway's' bearded mouth.

Lanny smiled to himself smugly, knowing now that the crippled professor was one of those scholarly men that lusted for man-play. He clung to the top of the partition as he pressed his hairy belly against the cool marble.

"Come on ol' Daddy," he thought. *"Feed your face."* The professor's expert mouth engulfed and siphoned Lanny's cock. He pressed himself harder against the partition, trying to absorb every morsel of sensation. He felt the intense suction, the wet sloshing of hot throat muscles, and whimpered. Even after just talking to the man, he couldn't believe this wheelchair bound professor of Anthropology was here now sucking his cock like a common dirty bookstore whore.

The sensation and the whole unbelievable scenario was too much for Lanny; he was on the brink of dumping a load of red neck dick spit down the throat of a university educated professor when the man abruptly stopped.

"Why don't you come over here and let me get at you better," he suggested.

Breathing hard and just barely able to contain his

orgasm, Lanny withdrew his spit soaked cock and pulled up his coveralls. At the other stall, he got the wheelchair out of the way and stepped inside. It was larger and roomier, designed to accommodate men like Owen.

"Turn around!" the professor said. "Now drop your coveralls and let me see your ass!" Lanny slowly let his coveralls fall, allowing the man to get a good look. He stood with hairy legs bent slightly, pinching both his nipples. "Now step back and bend over!" the professor ordered. Lanny turned, bent over and pushed out his hairy ass.

"This what y'all want?" he teased.

"Oh yeah, that's nice," the professor hissed. Lanny felt the man's strong hands lightly caressing his ass. "Damn, your ass is hairy," the big professor said. Lanny could feel the professor's beard tickling and his hot breath. He closed his eyes and felt the tongue snake its way closer to his pucker hole, then greedily trying to lap its way in. He moaned as the sensation overtook him. It felt so incredible that Lanny pushed his ass out further. He felt the professor spread his ass cheeks apart, then his finger probe lightly. "God, you're tight!" the professor said.

"Dang, Professor," Lanny whimpered. "You keep that up 'n I'm gonna' bust a nut fer sure."

After a few moments of finger fucking Lanny, the professor backed off and instructed Lanny to turn back around and face him. Between his legs, his thick uncut cock stood oozing, ready for attention.

"This gonna' satisfy that itch?" the older man said, grinning. Lanny couldn't stop his own greedy smile from spreading across his rugged face as he knelt down on the cold marble floor between the professor's thin, hairy legs.

"I never in a hundred years would a' thought I'd be doin' this," he confessed. After inhaling the wheel-bound professor's cock, he closed his eyes as the familiar taste of foreskin filled his mouth. Lanny bobbed his head slowly and suckled, savoring every veiny inch. All the while the professor cooed and stroked the janitor's close-cropped hair.

After exchanging teasing blowjobs, Lanny stood and removed his coveralls entirely; now he was dressed only in a worn sleeveless tee and work boots. The professor looked up admiring the ruggedly handsome man before him and a broad smile washed across his face. He appreciated this type of man; roughly simple and unassuming. He was the polar opposite of the white-collar nerds he was used to.

"What a beautiful body you have," he said reaching out his hands. Lanny stepped closer, allowing the professor's soft but burly hands to smoothly pass over his taut stomach and up across the hair covered pectorals. Lanny in turn slid his strong calloused hands over the professor, appreciating the well developed arms and the bulging biceps that were like iron. He maneuvered his hands under the professor's shirt and slipped it off. His broad shoulders were powerful and hairy as well.

Owen wrapped his strong arms around Lanny and inhaled deeply; the scent was a musky mixture of sweat, spicy aftershave and gear grease. He pulled the janitor closer, pressed his moist lips to the man's hard nipples and bit them softly.

"Dang!" Lanny cried out. He arched his back and straddled the big man's legs. Against his low hanging nuts, he felt Owen's cock liberally oozing its natural lube. He reached back and swabbed the hooded member along his taint, and finally against his furry butthole.

The assault on his nipples was electrifying, adding to his excitement. It was making rational thought impossible as deliciously nasty thoughts and images filled his head.
Professor Hardaway pawed at Lanny's back, pulling him down onto his cock.

"Oh, God, yes, please," he begged as though he'd never get a chance like this again. Lanny was only reluctant for a moment, surprisingly wanting it as much as Owen. He looked down at the broad shouldered man and thought this was something he never imagined he'd do. It was so wicked doing it in the museum, and somehow perverted getting fucked by the professor in a wheelchair.

"Yeah, give it to me fucker!" Lanny cried feeling the professor's cock stretch his sensitive ass lips. He exhaled softly; a mix of moan and breath as it slowly penetrated his butt hole and sank up into his insides.

The professor held on, clutching Lanny tight. All the while his ravenous mouth gnawed up Lanny's sensitive neck and chin, ultimately finding his bruised lips. As if possessed by demons, the professor clawed at Lanny's back, ripping at the worn material and finally tearing off his sleeveless tee. Lanny kissed back pressing his lips roughly against the professor's mouth. They were like two deranged men; each intent on consuming the other. Tongues meshed and teeth clashed as they crushed one another. Lost in an uncontainable frenzy of sexual pleasure; Lanny accidentally bit the professor's soft lips, drawing a trickle of blood. The professor lost in his own rapture didn't notice. Spit drooled and sweat dripped as hard man-flesh fought to take control. Lanny bore down as Owen pushed up, each absorbed in pleasure. Their clash grew rougher and their groans louder as they neared their climax. Lanny held on as the assault on his innards seemed unending. The professor rumbled like a rutting bull, thanked the gods for the feeling he did have, and bucked up harder.

"Yeah give it to me!" Lanny encouraged. They held on, going faster and harder until the professor pushed once and twice then finally groaned long and loud. Lanny felt the cock fixed deep inside expand and spew out its scalding mucus. But before the professor's convulsions settled, Lanny let go. He groaned deeply, and in typical Arkansas fashion, spewed forth a litany of blasphemous ravings as string after string of cum exploded onto the professor's robust chest and belly. Finally he collapsed against the satisfied professor, their hairy chests mixing with the result of their midnight tryst.

After a moment, with the musky scent of sweat and sperm lingering in the air, the echoes of spent cries died down, and like the silence after thunder, the marble walls of the men's room were eerily quiet. Lanny felt the professor's heart synchronized with his own, the loud beat slowing with each pulse. He lifted his head, looked down to the professor and realized he must be heavy.

"Professor?" he asked quietly but the professor didn't respond. "Hey buddy, yah still with me?"
Professor Owen Hardaway opened his glazed eyes and still didn't say anything. After a moment he said, unflinching,

"I think you've broken my legs."

"What?" Lanny gasped and jumped off, the big man's softening cock slipping out with a plop.

"Yeah, and I don't think I can walk," Owen added.

"What?" Lanny repeated, but more puzzled then before.

Owens' face lit up and the twinkle returned to his blue eyes and he smiled.

"Just kidding," he said.

"Dang Professor, yah almost had me going there fer a minute," he said, and then picked up the remnants of shredded cloth that was once his undershirt.

"Oh, sorry about that," the professor said meekly. Lanny held up and examined the tattered material.

"Ain't no big thing," he said tearing it further in two pieces. "It was only hangin' on by a couple of threads anyways."

Lanny bent close to the professor and wiped away the mess he'd left.

"Well, looks like there was a mess I had to clean up fer you after all," he smiled.

After they dressed and Owen was back in his chair, they said their goodbyes, and Lanny disappeared down the dark hall. He knew there'd be the occasional message about spills in the Anthropology Department, and he was sure the professor would be the one calling. Night duty wasn't so bad after all.

~

TO PROTECT AND SERVE

"Fuck!" I growled, when I noticed the red flashing lights in my rear view mirror. I had just gotten off Lake Shore Drive and was going through the park along the lake between Montrose and Foster Avenue.

After pulling over and stopping, I got out of my van and headed toward the squad car. I'd seen the officer before sitting in his cruiser off by himself. We'd nod to one another on occasion, but I'd never actually talked to him. Some of the men I'd gotten to know from coming here told me he was a protector of sorts. They said he'd sit and watch, even if you were doing someone, he wouldn't interrupt. Sometimes, he'd watch me go by, knowing full well I had just given or gotten a blow job. Only this time he stopped me and I was concerned he was finally going to arrest me.

I walked up as he was putting on his cap; we met just behind my van.

"Is there a problem officer?" I asked in my most charming voice; wanting to be polite as possible, knowing full well Chicago cops could be real dicks if they wanted to.

The officer approached me, and I realized he was much bigger then I had expected. He had a beautiful head of silver hair and neatly trimmed beard. He stood looking down at me and smiled, showing those manly crow's feet at the corners of his pale gray eyes. Even for a man of seemly advanced age, he wasn't bad looking.

I have always liked uniforms, especially police, and now I was getting an eye full. As he drew closer I could hear the creak of his leather jacket as he moved.

"Excuse me, sir. Looks as though one of your tail lights is out," he said while pointing to my brake light. And then to my astonishment, he looked down to my crotch. I was so surprised; I didn't know what to say. There was no mistaking his gaze. He put his big hands on his holster, and together with his pants, pulled them up. I couldn't help noticing the obvious bulge in his dark blue slacks. The polyester stretched across his crotch, giving me a very impressive view of his 'weapon'. I looked up and saw that he was still smiling. I tried to think of something to say but I just stuttered, "Umm, well I…"

"I can't permit you to drive that way," he said. "I'll have to follow you home. Just to make sure nothing happens," he added. With his left hand still on his holster, he tipped his cap back with his right.

"He's trying to seduce me," I thought to myself. Is this what entrapment was? If it was, I was going for it like a fly goes to garbage.

I jumped back into my old van and started for home. It didn't take long, as I live less than 10 minutes away. After parking in front, I got out and headed for the cruiser.

"Thank you, sir," I said. "I'll make sure I get that light fixed as soon as possible."

He looked at me again, then down to my tight, worn 501's.

"I better make sure you get in alright," he said smiling.

"Uh, all right," I said, still quite bewildered. At this point, I started to get seriously nervous, maybe I was reading this all wrong.

After getting into the house, I turned to face him and asked if he wanted something to drink. He looked even bigger standing there in the entrance way. He turned slightly to the left, and in his authoritative attitude, wiggled a finger at me.

"Come here!"

"Scuze me?" I asked.

"Come here!" he repeated while pointing to a spot on the floor before him. Nervously, I approached. He put one big hand on my shoulder and pulled me close. I could smell the scent of worn leather from his jacket as he looked down to me.

"I've been watching you, and since as I know I can trust you, I'd like some of this action you've been giving away." Slowly, he lowered his face down to mine and looked deeply into my eyes. I felt very small in his arms. Then he closed his eyes and kissed me. Almost immediately, he shoved his tongue down my throat. I couldn't believe this was happening; I tensed in his strong embrace.

"Relax, stud. I'm not going to hurt you. I have to make sure you're not carrying any concealed weapons," he joked. "I've been watching you," he repeated.

"You're a hot little fucker!" He kissed me again as I melted into his arms. I had fantasized about this and now it was really happening.

As he held me, I felt his hard stomach against mine. The scent of worn leather filled my nostrils at the same time the taste of coffee and doughnuts saturated my mouth.

He was the kind of man we all dream about and try to be like. He represented power and authority and I was giving in easily. His big arms wrapped around me, crushing my imaginary resistance. If this was the way to go, then I was going gladly. I felt him cup both meaty hands onto my ass. His mouth found my neck and bit down. I gasped for breath like a guppy out of water. Then he squatted down and I felt him fumble with the buttons of my fly. With both hands, he ripped opened my jeans, freeing my rising cock.

"No underwear, huh?" He pressed his face to my crotch. I felt his hot breath against my hardening cock.

"Uncut," he concluded. "I thought you might be. Finally, I get to taste this, and perfect size too."

"Thanks," I said, feeling a little self conscious.
He pulled my foreskin forward, and then with his tongue, he swabbed the head.

"Mmmm! I love foreskin," he confided. "I don't get to do this much." Not believing this was happening to me, I watched as he swallowed my cock. Here I was standing in my foyer, and kneeling in front of me was one of Chicago's finest, in full uniform. I put my hands on his shoulders, enjoying the sensation. My fingers ran across the well toned leather of his ebony jacket. Boldly, I pulled his head towards my crotch. I felt my cock bury itself in his hot throat. He gagged, but didn't back off. His big hands groped my ass cheeks, pulling me closer, while his mouth pressed tightly to my crotch. After a minute, he backed off, needing air.

"Whooie!" the cop gagged, tears in his eyes, and smiled. "I could swallow you whole." He wiped his mouth as he stood up. "Why don't we get comfortable?"

I suggested we go up to my bedroom. He walked in before me, turned around, told me to sit on the bed, and knelt before me again.

"Ok, get up and turn around." I could see our reflection in the mirror at the head of the bed. He began by taking my shirt off, then my jeans.

"Man, you've got a nice little hairy body! Get back on the bed on your hands and knees!"

Assuming the position, I was on all fours, my ass towards him. In the mirror I saw him pull out his night stick, then with it between my legs; he tapped my inner thighs, indicating he wanted me to spread them wider. I felt him slide the pseudo phallic symbol across my back.

"Lower your head down, ass up," he ordered. He brushed his big hand across my ass. "You do have a hairy butt, don't you?" I was about to answer yes, but before I could, I felt him shove his face into my ass. I gasped. It felt wonderful, feeling his tongue probe and explore. I squirmed as he tongue fucked me. I felt him pull at the tufts of ass hair too as I looked in the mirror, enjoying the show.

He devoured my ass for a while before getting up and beginning to disrobe. I sat back and watched as the big cop started to strip.

"I know some of you boys go in for uniforms, so I'll take it slow," he said as he placed his cap on my head.

"Could you leave your holster on?" I asked.

"Sure, if you'd like?"

"Yes sir." His jacket was beside me on the bed. The rest of his clothes were in a heap on the floor. As he stood there, I reached up and ran my hands through his chest hair. I explored his chest; nipples and hard belly then brought my hand down and let it linger on his holster

"Careful, boy," he warned. "That's a mighty powerful weapon and I wouldn't want you to get hurt." As he said this, a strange thrill ran through me. The thought of his gun so close to me was exciting.

"Can I touch it?" I asked feeling like a little boy asking his father for permission. I lightly traced the cold metal of the handgun with my fingers. I'd never seen a gun this close let alone held one, also I was surprised at its weight for its size.

Then we traded places; him on the bed and me on the floor. I held onto his holster as I brought my face to his crotch. I wanted to make this as memorable for him as it was for me. I buried my nose into his pubic hair as I took as much of his cock into my mouth as I could.

"Oh Lord!" he sighed. I siphoned his cock for some long minutes until he was at the brink.

"Oh, fuck, son. I'm gonna' shoot!" Immediately, I pulled off; I didn't want him to cum just yet. By this time, he was lying back on the bed, and I moved my mouth lower to his heavy balls, then licked and sucked them. I tongued his inner thighs as it drove him closer. I moved even lower as I lifted his thick legs.

"Oh, fuck!" he moaned. "Yeah!"

My tongue lapped at his muscular, hairy ass: now it was my turn to tongue-fuck him. He was mumbling almost incoherently, as I licked, lapped, and slurped.

"Come on, Officer," I pleaded. "Get on your knees and let me really get at it." I was in a better position to do a proper job and continued to service him.

"Oh, yeah, punk, suck my hole," he growled. I could tell he was enjoying this as much as I was.

"Ok, you little fuck," he said while pushing out his ass and looking back to me. "You got me, now fuck me!"

Kneeling behind him, I prepared to take him dog-style. As I said, he was big and his ass was somewhat high for me, so I had to pull him down to meet my cock. I inserted my uncut cock slowly as he closed his eyes.

"Ooooh" he sighed. My cock felt like it was literally being sucked in. I held onto his holster, using it for leverage as I mounted him. Then with my cock firmly planted, I fucked him. As I got comfortable, I got my rhythm and fucked him harder, I plunged deeper, making him groan. All the while he watched the mirror; seeing himself being fucked, being used. He was leaning on his elbows with his ass up and me behind. I didn't know if I had enough to satisfy this Daddy cop, but I was going to give it my best shot.

Because of his overall height, this position was getting a little tiring for me. Reluctantly, I pulled out and told him to get on his back. With much effort, I lifted his heavy, thick legs over my shoulders. At first I thought, how funny it must look; this big guy getting fucked by one smaller. But he seemed to be enjoying it, and I sure as damn well was too.

He pulled my body to his, then pushed his face against mine and kissed me. We kissed long and hard, enjoying our tongues in each other's mouths. I still couldn't believe this was really happening. Fucking this big cop was taking every bit of strength that I could muster. The weight of his lower body was almost more than I could hold up for any amount of time. If I ever thought about fucking a bull, this was as close as I was going to get.

I held onto his shoulders, pushing his legs up as far as I could, at the same time thrusting my cock in.

"Oh yeah, fuck my ass, boy!" he kept saying.

"You like fucking a policeman's ass?" he teased.

"Yes sir!" I answered.

"Come on, little stud; fuck my ass hole!" I looked into his gray eyes as I felt my orgasm rise inside me.

"Oh, fuck. I'm going to cum!" I told him.

"Oh yeah, baby! Do it!" he said as he pulled me even closer. I felt my balls pull up tight. The warm wet feeling around my cock grew tighter as it pushed through his sensitive anal lips. The sensation was incredible as my cock erupted.

I fell beside him panting, trying to catch my breath. He turned to me and started to get up.

"Ok, baby," he said, "its Daddy's turn!" I thought he was going to fuck me, but instead he straddled my chest. With my face between his thighs, his cock dripped pre-cum. He placed it against my lips and lifted my head to it.

"Suck it, boy! Do it like you did fucking my ass." I opened my mouth and did my best, but in this position, it was difficult. After much slobbering and gagging, he continued to jack off while I devoured his full-size nut sack.

"Oh yeah, that's it. I'm cumming'! Take it. Take it!" I opened my mouth waiting for the flow to start. He pumped his cock as he held my head, but I got more than I bargained for. This cop came in gallons; in my mouth, on my face and in my hair. Man, it went everywhere; thick and musty. After he was done, he brought his face to mine and kissed me again, then licked at my moustache, tasting his own cum.

After we finished and he was done dressing he looked at me seriously.

"Ok, son, I'm taking you in!" he said. Suddenly I froze.

"What?" I asked.

"Yeah, I'm taking you in. For being such a good fuck. I'm taking you in; into my ass and mouth, anytime we can get together," he said smiling.

"Man, you had me going," I told him. We hugged and kissed, and as I watched him drive away, I hoped there would be more times like this. And somehow I felt a little safer knowing he was out there; protecting and serving.

~

SUMMER OF LOVE

The late November sky loomed overhead, dark and moody, on the verge of showering me with hail. The old cemetery was quietly cold as I stood there alone and gathered my coat around me, hoping to keep the cold away. I looked down to the grave in front of me while dead leaves blew about my feet. My newly placed wreath seemed curiously out of place among the litter of long dead flowers. The oversized headstone with its icons of angels bore the name Peterson. Below was inscribed, "Matthew, Beloved Husband and Father."

Suddenly, I heard the cry of a crow; it was a mournful sound but so typical this time of the year. I looked and

caught sight of it high atop the old tree where we as kids
used to play, but most importantly, the place where I got my
first male-to-male kiss. I walked toward the tree as the crow,
dark against the sooty sky, eyed me with curiosity. Looking
to where I thought it would be, just above my head among
so many others, were the initials, M.P. + N.M. I thought it
funny; they meant nothing to any living soul but me. I
traced the long healed engraving in the bark with my gloved
finger, remembering what they meant. Despite the cold air,
a warm feeling came over me.

I remembered as if were yesterday, I was young then and
I had a hopeless crush on the young cemetery grounds
keeper; "Matthew, beloved husband and father." Only then
he was neither.

It was the summer of 1969 and would come to be known
as the "Summer of Love". But it was a tumultuous time as a
disillusioned young generation struggled to find its place.
Hippies clashed with the establishment while preaching free
love and flower power. Turn on, tune in, and drop out was
the catch phrase. The first man had just walked on the moon
and me; on the brink of manhood.

My family lived on the edge of town, close to the
cemetery. My friends and I would usually pass through it on
our way to the woods. One day, I saw him for the first time.

It was a beautiful summer day, full of birds chirping and a blue sky full of cottony alabaster clouds. He had just gotten out of a beat up Volkswagen van, painted with peace signs and flowers. The AM radio was playing "Momma told me not to come", by Three Dog Night. The first thing I noticed was his mop of golden hair, streaked by sunshine with highlight upon highlight of dark yellow to platinum. He was a blond giant with skin the color of spring break. His eyes, even at the distance I was standing, were brilliantly blue like Mediterranean waters. At that moment, I'd never seen a more handsome man.

He was usually shirtless and always wore low-rise sneakers. Most of the times he'd wear cut off shorts with the pockets dangling down, white against his hairy, copper colored legs, while he rode his tractor back and forth. I loved seeing him that way because he looked naked, and I wonder just how hairy his crotch was. Sometimes he'd wave to me; I suppose he got used to seeing me there.

One hot afternoon I'd gotten the idea to take along an extra soda, thinking he might want it. I actually got up the nerve to offer it to him, and he accepted. He sat atop his mower, head tilted back with his hairy legs opened wide, as if just for me. Sometimes he was vulgar and used words like fuck, shit or piss. Now I realize he was just trying to impress me.

In one corner of the cemetery was an old tool shed with an outhouse at one side. It was in need of repair and paint, not to mention smelly. Inside there were old nudie magazines that had some pages stuck together. Dirty graffiti and poorly drawn pictures of people having sex covered the grimy walls. A couple of the pictures were clearly of men sucking and getting fucked. Sometimes I'd sit there with the pretense of taking a shit, but actually I'd be peeking through one of the many holes in the walls at Matt on his mower and jacking myself to a wet mess.

One afternoon I got to the cemetery only to find Matt talking to an older woman. She had over-processed platinum blond hair, stiff from too much hairspray and held a cigarette elegantly between two red tipped fingers. She wore a tight, flowery summer dress, too short for her age and on her face was a large pair of dark sunglasses. Occasionally she'd laugh loudly and pat her cotton candy hair over and over as if to keep it in place.

She was obviously a woman of some importance, as you could tell by the huge Cadillac that was parked just a few yards away. I watched in fascination from the old tree as she looked around and laid her hand on Matt's knee then whispered something into his ear. Even from where I stood I could see him turn beet red. He looked at his watch, and then looked around to see if anyone was watching.

I ducked behind the tree, and when I looked again, I saw them walking to the tool shed. I waited until they were inside before deciding to follow. I had to see what they were going to do, although I had a pretty good idea.

I sneaked to the shed and entered the outhouse side, quiet as I could be, even holding my breath. I sat down and put my ear to the wall that separated the two spaces. I could hear them whispering and her giggling, then silence. Through a tiny hole I could see them; Matt's back was to me, and she was in front of him. Her hands were on his back as she held him tight. My emotions rose as I watched. I was excited but jealous; I hated them both, especially her.

I saw her hands slip down to his ass and squeeze. Then to my amazement she lowered his shorts, exposing his beautiful ass. Her gaudy red painted fingers felt his ass cheeks. I heard him moan. That's when I realized what was happening; she was on her knees sucking his cock. Now I really hated her. I was mad at them, but I also wanted to see.

"Oh baby, you're a big boy!" She said. Then I heard her mouth filled moaning. I groaned in return. Why couldn't it be me in there with him? I was so jealous; I stopped looking and sat back away from the wall. I squeezed my crotch and thought, wondering what to do.

Suddenly, the door behind me burst open with a whoosh. The flash of midday sun momentarily blinded me.

There at the door was the bubble haired Medusa, with red smeared lips and glaring at me. Before I could react, she violently grabbed me by the arm and pulled me out.

"You sneaky little pervert!" she screamed. "Who sent you here?"

"No one, I was just using the toilet," I said looking from her to Matthew.

"You liar, you were spying. How dare you spy on me?" Her words shot out like venom, as my ears burned with embarrassment.

"No I wasn't, let me go."

Behind her was Matthew, hastily fastening his zipper and anxiously looking around.

"Shh!" he hissed bouncing a finger against his lips. "Don't yell so loud; someone's gonna hear you," he pleaded.

She abruptly turned to face him, and with me still in her grasp, slapped him hard across the face. Stunned and speechless, he stared at her in wide-eyed disbelief, holding his reddening cheek.

"Don't you ever tell me what to do!" she spat. "No one tells me what to do! Understand?"

"Let me go!" I said breaking the tension. Then she turned her wrath on me and slapped me as well. I held my cheek as I felt the tears well up in my eyes, but I wasn't going to cry, not in front of Matthew and especially not in front of her.

"Shut up you little faggot!" Her words hit me harder that the slap she'd just given me. Embarrassed, I tried not to look at Matthew.

"What do you think you were doing?" she hissed. "Is this what you wanted to see?" She asked while grabbing at Matthew's crotch.

"Let him go, you bitch," he said pushing her hand away. With her attention diverted, I felt her hold on me let up. I wiggled out of her red-clawed grasp and ran.

"Come back here you!" she screamed after me.

I zigzagged through the head stones, almost tripping but only once did I look back. I saw them arguing, her storming to her car, and then finally speeding away, throwing loose gravel and dirt in her wake. My heart was pounding as I tried to catch my breath. I felt as though I had just barely gotten away with my life.

By the time I got home, I was so filled with rage and shame that I had to wait for myself to calm down before going into the house.

"That bitch!" I repeated Matthew's words. That night in bed I replayed the wretched incident over in my mind, still feeling my cheek burn red. It was a while before I finally got to sleep. Even then, I had troubling dreams.

Days later I thought about going back to see him, but I couldn't bring myself to. I was still too embarrassed but eventually my libido overcame reason and I found myself at the gates of the cemetery. I was freshly washed and wearing new shorts which were obscenely too small. Again I brought along an extra soda, hoping Matthew might be thirsty. I could hear the tractor's engine off to the west. I walked towards the sound, not knowing what to expect. Finally I saw him riding in my direction. He was busy concentrating on his job, but managed to see me and waved. My heart skipped a beat thankful he wasn't mad at me. He came to a stop, turned off the engine and got down from the seat. Only he didn't come my way. Instead, he headed toward the tool shed. I thought it funny that he would wave to me then walk away. As he got to the shed, he turned around, smiled and winked at me. Then he did something I wasn't sure of; it looked as though he squeezed his crotch. A thrill ran through me. I stood there not knowing what to do. Was this some kind of cruel joke? Was it a trap?

After a few long minutes, I decided to go see what he was up too, so I quietly entered the outhouse side. The memory of the Medusa walking in on me filled me with dread, so I made sure to lock the door.

I headed straight for the wall where the holes were. I kneeled, being careful not to get my shorts dirty and looked, but at first, I didn't see him. Then he came into view. He crossed the room while taking his shirt off, and then sat down on another tractor. I watched in fascination as he passed his hand slowly over his body. His fingers flicked his nipples, one hand slid down and over his flat belly, following the line of fine, wispy hairs. Then he popped open the top button of his cut offs. I sucked in a short breath watching him slowly and purposely lowering his zipper. Beads of sweat appeared below his nose.

Once his zipper was down completely, he stood up and turned away from me. I watched in anticipation as he lowered his shorts, exposing his beautiful, white ass. It had a fine covering of curly hair. I groped myself. Suddenly he turned sideways and his cock came into view. I gasped again. I'd wanted to see it since first setting eyes on this blond hunk, and now here it was in all its magnificence. It was as white as his sun-protected butt with foreskin that covered only half the head. Slowly and lovingly, he slid his hand down and up its length. I was close enough to see the blue-purple veins running across its surface. At its base was an abundance of wiry, pale red hair.

His balls hung loosely in their protective pouch like two eggs in a silken bag. With his thumb, he pushed his cock down away from his body. Letting it go, it sprang up and slapped loudly against his taut belly. He did this twice. Then he held it out and he bent over. I watched in disbelief as his tongue snaked out and lightly licked his cock head. Then he did something unexpected; he turned his head, looked in my direction and smiled.

He then curled one finger and wiggled it at me. In the quiet of the hot tool shed he whispered,

"Come here!" I froze. He knew I was looking. I felt my face flush with embarrassment, and bolted upright. I sat there not knowing what to do. Slowly I leaned over and looked again.

"Please!" he added. Slowly I stood up, and in a trance, I walked around to the other side of the tool shed. My heart pounded with excitement and anticipation as I opened the door slowly. I was mesmerized by the sight of him sitting atop the tractor without a stitch of clothing except for his torn sneakers. His long legs were spread open obscenely inviting me in.

Inside the tool shed it was hot and stuffy. The smell of grease and oil, mixed with the smell of dried grass filled my nostrils. The closer I got to him, the more I could feel the heat from his body. He smelled of cocoa butter, sweat and salt all mixed together. It wasn't altogether unpleasant. His blue eyes bored into me as he stroked his cock.

"Take your shirt off." He said in a hoarse whisper. I obeyed. Then he held out his hand to me. It was only then that I realized this was the first time we'd actually touched. The electricity of the moment passed up my arm and throughout my body, then right down to my crotch. At that moment I knew he was all mine, but what I hadn't realize then was that I was totally his, and ready to do whatever he asked of me.

I tossed my shirt aside as he watched with hungry eyes. All the while his hand slowly, lovingly slid up and down the impressive length of his magnificent tool. It looked incredibly hard, almost painful and I couldn't take my eyes off it.

"I knew you were watching," he said finally. "I didn't think she'd find out or get so mad. She's an old bitch anyway."

"Uh huh," I said, but that was all I could manage to say.

"I like being watched," he admitted.

I stood between his open legs with my hands resting on his hairy thighs. I could feel the sensual heat coming from his crotch like a furnace.

"Feel my balls," he said as he held them out for me. They were incredibly hot and hung low, hiding his asshole from me. I reached out to hold them as he closed his eyes in rapture as. Then he put his hand on my shoulder and gently pulled me closer.

He wanted me to bend over. I gave in and leaned down until his balls were close to my lips.

"Lick them," he whispered. My tongue flicked out and I heard him moan. I licked and sucked at his balls, enjoying the feel and texture. I tried greedily to put both of them into my mouth, but found I couldn't. His cock lay back hard and long against his belly, I couldn't take my eyes off it. It was one of those fat cocks with a thick cord running along the underside.

His ass was even with my chin, and sometimes I'd swab my tongue just low enough under his balls to lightly pass it over his pucker hole. Whenever I did that, he'd jerk up and groan. But I wanted to taste his cock.

"Oh, yeah!" he groaned. So I reached up and took it into my hand while his glazed over blue eyes watched me as I brought it to my lips. At its head was a clear drop of pre-cum, I licked at it and it stuck to my tongue. For a moment we were tied by this spider web string of life. Without thinking and without shame, I brought it to my mouth.

His cock was velvety smooth but also like a steel spike; hard and pulsed with each beat of his heart. My lips slid up and down over its head.

"Oh, fuck!" he groaned. "Your mouth is so hot." He held my head with both hands as he used my mouth. Drool dribbled down my chin and onto my chest. The sounds of my slobbering filled the small space. If anyone were to walk by just then, they would have known exactly what was going on. Suddenly I thought about the bubble-haired Medusa. In self-satisfied smugness, I smiled to myself despite the fat cock that was lodged down my throat. With all her power and connections, I had what she wanted.

I looked up at him and watched his lean muscular chest heaving up and down. Then I noticed his armpits and how the hair there was wet with sweat. It dripped down his sides. His blond hair was also matted against his forehead. The combination of smells: the oil, the grease, and the musky scent of his crotch and ass were intoxicating. Not to mention the feel of his thick, alabaster cock sliding across my tongue and down my throat, all in that little space, made my head spin. Through watery eyes I watched him in awe.

Then he grabbed the seat of the old tractor with both hands and braced himself. I knew he was heading for a climax. He had a look of complete concentration as he stared at the ceiling. Eager to please him, I bobbed my head faster onto his cock. I didn't know what would happen after this was over, but I wanted him to want more, so I was doing my best to give him pleasure.

Sometimes I'd swallow his cock as far down my throat as I could manage. Other times, I'd run my hand just ahead of my mouth, sliding it over his spit covered cock. I was enjoying this too and suddenly realize the power I had over him. Here I was; younger and skinnier, but I had him where I wanted. I had the awesome power to make him moan and quiver with delight.

His body quaked with the onslaught of his approaching orgasm. He stopped for a second then came with a grunt that turned into a long drawn out moan. I felt his spunk wash over my tongue, tasting salty and sweet all at the same time. It filled my mouth and I swallowed gulp after gulp as I fought to hold on, with me heaving and bouncing all the way. All through this I jacked myself off, then with the taste of his cum fresh on my lips, I came. Rope after rope covered the base of the old tractor as I shook and gasped.

After it was over, I realized we were both soaking wet, and we laughed together for no reason other than feeling foolishly absurd.

We got dressed and got out of the little hot shed. Outside there was a pump where we could wash off. I watched him still marveling at his taunt muscles.

It went on this way throughout the summer, sometimes going further with our love making, and other times, just mutual masturbation. Luckily, the bubble haired Medusa never did materialize again to torment us. We heard she divorced her husband and moved out west. Finally, just before school was to start, we met for what was to be the last time.

It was early evening and we met under the old tree. The sky was rapidly turning dark, and the last of the cicadas had come and gone. Summer had ended, and so had our time. He told me that he had to go back to college and wouldn't see me for a while. I was sad, but glad for the time we had. He came closer and took me into his arms, looked deeply into my eyes, then kissed me. It was a long, passionate kiss, and he did something I'd only heard about; he used his tongue like lovers in movies do.

I was surprised but responded by holding him tighter; I didn't want to let him go. It was then that I realized that this was it; there would be no other times like this. Then he peeled himself away from me and said goodbye, got into his old beat up Volkswagen van, waved one last time, and drove off. I watched as the glow of his taillights disappeared beyond the cemetery gates.

Later that night, I came back and carved our initials into the old tree. I wanted to remember this forever... as if I would ever forget.

~

MR. TUCKER

"Where's he gonna' sleep?" I heard Alex's Dad ask. Alex and his family lived a couple of streets from my house. They were one of the few black families that lived on this side of town, and we knew each other from the neighborhood. After finding out we were both interested in guitars, we became friends. Our fantasy was to form a rock group and make it big. Needless to say, it never happened.

"He can sleep in my bed," Alex insisted.

"What about your brothers?"

"Maybe they can sleep in the basement, on that old sofa bed?"

"No, they can't. I'm gonna' be down their tonight," he said wistfully. "Your momma's in a snit."

Mr. Tucker wasn't a very tall man, but big in any case, with wide shoulders. Forty seemed so old to me back then but he was actually younger than my dad.

He was the type of black man that was very hairy and losing his hair. His lips were what you'd call voluptuous and the dark hair on his body made him look even darker. He was fascinating to look at and I found him very interesting.

He thought for a while then said, "I guess you guys can sleep downstairs on the floor." Alex looked down to his feet, dejected.

"You can stay up later than usual," his father added.

"All right!" we cheered.

Early evening came and went. We were already sacked out in front of the TV, watching late night monster movies. Alex was beside me falling asleep. Mr. Tucker walked by on his way to the basement, off the kitchen.

"Good night, boys."

"Huh!" Alex woke up with a start.

"Oh, goodnight dad." Alex looked at me groggily and decided to sleep in his own bed with his brothers. After he left, I turned the TV off and sat there and thought about what I'd heard. The rumor was that all black men had very large dicks. I'd seen Alex's and I wasn't overly impressed.

Mr. Tucker, on the other hand, did show a pretty impressive bulge.

The house was quiet, just the occasional bark of a neighbor's dog or the sound of a passing car. I'd been lying there for a while thinking, mostly about Mr. Tucker, when I heard someone walk past. A dim light coming from the kitchen illuminated my face. I heard a noise like bottles clicking. Quietly, I tip-toed to the kitchen, peeking in just in time to see Mr. Tucker rise up from behind the refrigerator door and take out a bottle of beer. By the way he was weaving; I could see it wasn't his first. He was wearing an old pair of briefs, with leg openings too loose to be able to hold in his privates, and an equally tattered undershirt. After opening the bottle, he swung his head back and took a long, deep drink, then abruptly burped so loud he looked around, hoping he was indeed alone. He scratched himself and started back downstairs.

I followed him to the basement door, and from the dark stairway, I could hear him moving around, as though he was looking for something. The only light was from a small lamp that soon went off, and then I heard the sound of motorized clicking; it was a projector. I could tell by the dim flickering light, and I recognized the sound from school. I snuck down for a better look, but the weight of my foot made the step creek loudly.

"Alex?" I heard Mr. Tucker yell. I froze. "Alex is that you? I know you're there boy!" I had to answer.

"No Mr. Tucker it's me, Nick."
He didn't say anything at first, just silence.

"Oh," then a pause. "Get me another beer, will you boy?" I hurried back to the kitchen and returned to the same spot.

"Here you go Mr. Tucker," I said timidly.

"Bring it here, boy!" he slurred. Slowly and as quietly as I could, I proceeded down the dark stairs into the dimly lit basement.

"Over here!" he whispered. I could barely see him sitting on the old sofa bed, but I did notice the empty beer cans around him. I stood in front of him and handed him the beer.

"Where's Alex?" he asked as he took the bottle.

"He went to sleep with his room." I looked at the screen.

"You ever see fuck pictures boy?" The way he said the word fuck sent a shiver down my spine.

"Yes sir!" I answered, scared yet excited. "My uncle has lots."

On the screen was a white woman sucking a black man's cock. Neither one was remotely good looking. The woman was wearing a cheap blond wig, probably as a disguise. The man was extremely thin, and wearing only black socks. His cock was thin, rubbery, and not at all interesting. You could tell neither one was enjoying themselves.

"Might as well sit down and join me." I did as he suggested and sat on the other end of the old sofa. "Man, is she ug-lee, but she sure can suck a mean cock." I found the contrast between her white skin and the dark black cock quite erotic and started to get hard.

Just recently I had become curious about black men, often hearing they were supposed to be hung like horses. The black boys in school weren't promising examples. Looking at Mr. Tucker, I wondered what his cock was like.

Without looking at me, he told me to get a bottle of whisky from the shelf beside me. After searching a while, I couldn't locate it.

"It's not here, sir." I told him.

"Let me see."

After getting up he stood in front of me. The basement was small, so he was extremely close. His crotch was inches away. In the dim light of the projector, it looked enormous. Finding what he was looking for, he opened the bottle and drank deeply. His crotch was almost in my face as he drank, then he looked down at me and smiled.

"I know what you're thinking," he whispered. "You're wondering if mine's bigger than the guy's on the screen. Aren't you?" he asked while pointing back to the screen. "You ever see a black man's cock?"

His words echoed in my ears. I couldn't answer. I just kept staring; watching the thing in his white briefs getting larger and bigger as he loomed over me.

"Want to see it?" he asked. The question and the way he asked sent a shiver up my spine.

"Yes sir," I answered timidly while reaching out my hand.

"Go ahead. Pull 'em down."

Leaning forward, I placed my trembling fingers on the waistband of his underwear. Slowly, I lowered them, exposing more of his lower belly. His dark pubic hair glistened as though wet. Suddenly, his cock sprang up before my face, big, thick, and dark.

"Touch it, boy!" he commanded.

Licking my lips absentmindedly, I traced the bulging veins. It jumped when my fingers came in contact with the soft skin. And speaking of skin, he did have an ample amount of foreskin. His balls hung low, like two goose eggs within a velvet sack, sprinkled with ebony wiry hair.

I had sucked cock before. I was no virgin, by any means, but this was different. It wasn't only bigger; it was black and forbidden in those days; a big taboo. Races shouldn't mingle, I remembered. Maybe that's what turned me on the most, because I wasn't supposed to.

I placed my lips on the spongy head. It was warm and twitched at the slightest touch. With each lick, I watched it dance before my eyes.

"Go ahead boy, take in your mouth. I've heard you're pretty good at it," he teased. So, he had heard. I wondered who could have told him. I had my suspicions, but at the moment I really didn't care.

I grabbed his cock by its thick base as if it was a Billy club. It had a slightly musky smell. No doubt from being in underwear all day. I noticed the lush bush and the way the hair line traveled up his slight beer belly. Running my hand along his stomach, I realized it wasn't coarse at all, but soft and thick.

He grabbed my head as he pumped his cock into my mouth. I gagged at first; it was just too damn thick but soon found a comfortable rhythm. Occasionally I would choke, and spit would drip from my mouth, but I held on. I was moaning, enjoying the sensation of it all when he pulled out.

"Whooie boy, you sure can suck. You're better than the old lady." Then he did something unexpected; he knelt down in front of me and started feeling me.

"Ok, now it's your turn. It's only fair," he said while looking at me with those big, dark eyes. Because of his drinking, I wondered if he was going to remember any of this.

With one hand he softly pushed me back, with the other he pulled at my sweats. Then without fanfare, he lowered his head and engulfed my cock in one swallow. His mouth was hot, incredibly hot.

"Oh God," I whimpered. I could tell this was not his first time. I was getting the best blow job I had up until then. I don't know if it was the booze he had drunk or what, but he was giving me one hell of a blow job, and I was really enjoying it. He was grunting and slobbering. Man, he was hot. So was I for that matter. My head was thrown back, moving from side to side and I was moaning incoherently. I was on the verge of shooting my load. My balls came tight against my crotch, I was cumming.

"Mr. Tucker. I'm gonna' cum," I warned him. He kept going, only faster. Then a moan escaped from of my mouth.

It started low and intensified as cum spewed from my cock.
Mr. Tucker swallowed till I was spent, then he backed off
and quickly stood up. He jacked-off on me as I looked up at
him. His eyes were closed and I noticed a drop of cum at the
corner of his mouth. It looked so white against his dark skin
as it dripped down his chin. I looked down to his beautiful
cock just in time to see him shooting. It splattered my face,
my hair, and down the front of my chest. He stood there
pumping, draining every last drop. Then he straddled my
legs and kissed me. I welcomed his tongue. I had heard the
word voluptuous, but I didn't know quite what it meant
until now. That's what his lips were as they smothered mine.
He looked at me then kissed my cheek, patted my head and
told me to go to bed.

~

LOST DADDY

As with all dog owners, I was on my nightly "walking the dog" ritual. I walked along my usual route, down the alley behind my house. On my way back, I saw old Sean, the homeless man that hung around the neighborhood. Everyone in the area liked him. He was a friendly, likable guy, who never asked for anything and mostly kept to himself. I couldn't tell you how old he was, I imagined he was somewhere in his sixties. Because of his long white hair and full beard, he reminded me of Santa Claus, with a deep grandfatherly voice. I often wondered just what brought him to this hard life, where his family was, or even if he had one.

"Hi, Sean," I said. "How's business?"

He turned to me. "Good day to ya,'" he responded in a beautiful Irish brogue. "And how's the babies?" The babies were my dogs. The man loved dogs, and he really liked mine.

"Oh they're fine," I answered. There was something in his demeanor that always impressed me. He had his ever-present grocery cart and small dog with him.

"Hot evening wouldn't ya say?" he said.

I agreed, and it occurred to me that he might like to wash up.

"Sean, how does a shower sound?"

"A shower, oh, I'd dearly love that, sir." he said, looking at me as though I'd just offered him a million dollars.

"Why don't you park your cart in the yard and come in. The dogs can play together out here. As he walked into the yard, I realized just how baggy his clothes were.

"Oh, you have such a lovely home," he said in awe.

"Why don't we go upstairs, and you can jump in the shower," I said. "While you bathe, I'll wash your clothes if you'd like."

"Oh, sir, you're too kind. It's been many a day I wished for a saint like you."

"Sean, I'm hardly a saint. It's just that you remind me of someone I knew once." Immediately my grandfather came to mind. I put my hand on his shoulder, which was even with my face, and walked him upstairs. Once in the master bathroom, he noticed the whirlpool bath.

"Oh my word, I've never been in one of those," he confessed.

"I'll tell you what. After you finish your shower, you can enjoy the whirlpool. How's that sound?"

"You are a saint. These old weary bones could sure use it."

He began to strip, not caring if I was watching. I guess in all those shelters, one could not afford to be shy. He started with his shirt; a tattered old thing. My heart went out to him, as I stood there watching. Underneath, was a sleeveless tee-shirt, stained and ripped also. His broad shoulders were covered with white hair, as was his chest. I couldn't help but stare but looked away before getting to see his privates; not wanting to take advantage of this situation.

One by one, he handed me his clothes. They were so old and torn, that my first instinct was to throw them away. I was certain that's where he had gotten them in the first place. Luckily, I had some clothes, left behind by another large man that I knew would fit his large bulk.

Nearing the bathroom, I heard Sean singing. He had a wonderful, baritone voice. It was obvious he was enjoying his shower. Listening to him sing, I ran the water to the whirlpool. Sean poked his head out from behind the shower curtain, his hair and beard full of lather.

"It's just me, Sean." I said. "Incidentally, I found some clothes that might fit you." He looked at me sort of funny.

"Maybe you could use them or know someone who might." I could tell he was a proud man. He said nothing as he ducked his head back inside and continued to sing. Before long, the tub was full just in time as Sean pulled back the shower curtain, grabbed a towel and stepped out.

With him being so close and me still on my knees, I couldn't help but notice his cock. He was uncircumcised, and I wondered how big it would get. Sean looked at me then to his cock. He smiled but said nothing.

"I hope it's not too hot for you, Sean? Test it and see if it's ok." He leaned over and dipped his hand in. His cock was so close; I had to force myself not to reach out for it. I could sense that he knew what was going through my mind and he straightened up, with his cock still within reach, and patted my head.

"Oh, that's just dandy," he said. I felt his hand linger for a second. I stood up next to him, but not before noticing that his cock started to expand. He towered over me as I fought the urge to put my arms around him.

"You'd better get in before it gets cold."

He nodded. I watched as he climbed and lowered himself down into the steamy water with a sigh. A sigh that was low and deep, with just a hint of a rumble.

"Well, enjoy yourself," I said and started to leave.

"You're a fine saintly lad, and with all this water it would be a pity to waste it all on just me. I'd be honored if you'd join me." I couldn't believe my ears, but jumped at the chance.

"Well, if you don't mind, I think I will," I said, not wanting to sound too anxious. Sean watched with interest as I began to strip. Sitting on the edge of the tub, I let myself get used to the hot water. I felt his eyes on me as I sank into the tub. With closed eyes I sighed too, as though finally being able to relax. I opened them to see his eyes twinkling as they looked back at me; they were so blue and clear.

The tub was just big enough for the two of us. Even so, we could not help touching. We sat there up to our shoulders in the soothing water; below the bubbles I could feel his leg against mine.

"It sure'n does feel grand," he replied. I wondered if he meant the water or our hairy legs touching. I watched him laying there with his eyes closed, hair plastered to his forehead and his white beard floating before him, I realized what a good looking man he really was. He opened his eyes and looked at me, then gave me a big smile.

"*God,*" I thought, "*This man is melting my heart.*" He brought his big hand up to his neck and began to rub it.

"My goodness, I must have slept wrong last night," he murmured. I wondered where the poor old guy had slept.

"You got a kink in your neck, Sean?" I asked. "Why don't you turn around and let me massage it for you."

"Aren't you a nice man? You don't have to do that for old Sean."

"Oh, I don't mind," I practically begged. He agreed and turned to face away from me, then sat between my outstretched legs. I placed my hands on his hair covered shoulders and began to massage his thick neck. Immediately, he started to moan.

"Oh sir, you have the hands of a saint." His hands were at his sides, and on my legs. "You sure'n have powerful legs, sir." He said as he started to run his hands over them.

"Thank you, and stop calling me sir. Why don't you call me Nick, ok?

"I would be honored, Nicolas."

"Here, lie back and let me do your temples," I suggested.

"Oh sir, might I?"

"Nick!" I repeated. "Of course you can. I would enjoy it too. He leaned back onto me, his large frame almost covering me. Half his weight was on me as I massaged his temples and stroked his longish hair. All the while he cooed like a baby.

Soon, I was taking liberties; my touching was getting more deliberate and intimate. I couldn't believe this was happening. Here I was with a homeless man I'd found so interesting. I'm sure if my friends found out about this, they would think me crazy. But I was in heaven. I wanted to savor this moment. I stroked his beard, moving my hands lower to his hairy chest.

He really was a powerfully built old gentleman. My hands cupped his two large pectorals, then down further to his hard belly. I rubbed it while leaning my head against his. He was starting to breathe a little heavier.

"This is not fair of me to take advantage of you like this," I said feeling a little guilty. "Would you prefer I stop?"

"I would prefer to continue on like this. It's been a long time since I had the hands of a handsome man upon this old body. Sure'n I'd be lying if I told you I didn't favor it," He confessed.

"This old body is what I favor," I told him squeezing him slightly.

"Why don't you let me return the favor and lean your fine young body onto mine?" He asked as he turned around to face me.

After reversing positions, I found myself happily leaning against his brawny chest. Sean's big hands were all over my shoulders and chest, pinching my nipples. Every so often he would kiss the top of my head. I was in heaven leaning against this big man, purring like a kitten. I felt like a boy in my grandfather's arms so long ago.

"Do you like this son?" he whispered into my ear.

"Oh, yes," I answered, realizing our rolls were suddenly reversed. He kissed my ear.

"That's my boy." He whispered.

My hands caressed his hairy thighs, at the same time his granddaddy belly felt warm and wonderful against my back.

"Turn around and face me," he said. "I want to look at you." I did as I was ordered and with my legs over his, we looked into each others' eyes. With his hand on my shoulders he spoke.

"Listen, son. I'm an old man. I don't have a thing. No home, no family, nothing. You, you're handsome, you have a fine home. If anyone is taking advantage, it's me. Are you sure you want a raggedy old man like me?"

I pulled him closer and closed my eyes as our lips met. We embraced in a long, passionate kiss. His tongue filled my mouth as I greedily accepted it. This was what I wanted.

"Oh, Sean," I found myself saying. "Hold me in your arms. I want to be your boy for just a little while."

"Yes, you can be my boy; my handsome boy." Suddenly, he got up and sat on the edge of the tub.

I sat fascinated as I watched the water runoff his large hairy body. He moved as if in slow motion. His fat, uncut cock came into view. Beneath were two massive balls. The water ran off them in a single stream, and then he opened his legs wide. His cock was hard, but still hung low from its own weight. A small portion if his cock head was exposed. I leaned forward while supporting myself on his knees. Sean pulled me to his chest and held me.

"*Oh, how wonderful,*" I thought. I was kneeling between his hairy legs up and up against his hairy belly. I felt safe and warm; just like I did with my grandfather so many years ago. With our arms around each other, Sean rocked us back and forth.

"My Nicolas, my little Nicky." He said. "How I've wanted you. I never would have believed you would want an old homeless man like me. I should have been surer of myself." He pushed my head down to his chest and to his nipples.

"Kiss them, son." I licked and sucked them. They were large from years of play. He moaned and urged me on. "Suck them boy," he said in his Irish brogue. "But, I think we best be getting out. I have wrinkles enough."

I smiled and agreed. We dried each other, taking care and enjoying each other's bodies. Then, without warning, he picked me up and carried me to the bedroom and placed me gently, on the bed. He towered over me.

"Would you be a'wanting to suck my cock, now?" he asked me with a devilish look in his eye. I couldn't think of a thing in the whole world I'd rather do.

I grabbed his cock by its broad base and leaned forward, with mouth open. The head filled my mouth entirely and soon, I tasted the familiar taste of foreskin. I moaned a deep, satisfying moan as I pressed my head even further onto his magnificent cock.

"Oh my, you are a hungry lad, aren't you boy?"

"Mmph huh," I said. The head was slick with pre-cum. I savored the taste.

"You love cock! Don't you boy?"

"Yes sir!" I answered as I let go for an instant.

"I sure'n do love seeing my cock disappear into that handsome mouth of yours." I was now kneeling between his out-stretched legs. I had one hand just before my mouth, following my up and down strokes. He was in heaven as the room filled with the sounds of my sucking, gagging and Sean's moaning.

"Slow down boy!" he said. "I want this to last. I haven't had this much attention in a whole lot of years. Get on your back for a while. I want to feel the back of your throat." The old man positioned pillows behind my head, and then put his cock back into my mouth.

"Open up son; take this old daddy's cock."

Slowly, he began to shove his fat cock back and forth, fucking my mouth. This was where I wanted to be, at the mercy of some big man, force feeding his cock to me. He was holding my head with one hand as he shoved his cock into my face, over and over again. With each thrust I heard his grunts.

"That's it, take it boy! Eat your daddy's cock." Sean was in his own thoughts now. Using me and using my mouth. Suddenly without warning, he gave one last deep thrust and held it in me. He had his full weight on me, his whole cock embedded in my mouth. I realized he was cumming. I felt it pulse as it ejaculated.

"Yes, yes," he kept repeating. Then a deep growl, a growl so deep and low, that I swear I heard the windows vibrate. But just when I was ready to panic from the lack of air, he let go. I swallowed, finally tasting his cum and gasped for breath. Sean fell beside me; spent. It was then I realized I had shot too. My hairy belly was covered with it. It was one of the few times in my life that I had cum without touching myself. Soon, he was asleep and snoring softly. As I lay there content, listening to the sounds of the evening, and his rhythmic breathing, I had the feeling old Sean had found a home. I didn't know how long he would stay, or even if he wanted to. But I hoped it would be for long time.

~

BAR TALE

A chilly October rain drenched the city as I shifted my weight from one foot to the other, anxiously waiting for the shift to end. The bar was quiet; a few patrons peppered themselves here and there, hoping for that certain someone that would brighten their lives or at least; their afternoon. For me it was business as usual when another customer walked in.

At first glance I didn't think he looked old enough to be in the bar, but then he spoke.

"O'Doul's!" he said in a surprisingly deep voice. His thick black hair was closely cropped to his scalp and he had one of those fashionable chin beards you see all the boys wearing now. In his left eye brow, he sported a ring.

Ouch!" I thought to myself. His clothes were baggy and hung loose, hiding his build. He didn't look directly at me, but down, as if he was afraid to look at me. I don't think of myself as being intimidating to look at, but I've found some people see you entirely differently than you see yourself. I handed him his drink and said,

"Thank you, sir!" I sometimes find it funny calling a guy so much younger than myself sir, but I think they get a kick out of it.

He headed for the pinball machines and played several games, occasionally wandering out back to the patio and back in for another drink, each time tipping me a dollar. There was something about the kid that interested me, something I couldn't put my finger on, but he had a sexy manner about him. He wasn't what you'd call cute or handsome. On the contrary, he was just this side of ugly. But as I said he was sexy and had a manly swagger.

Finally my relief came in the form of the night bartender. I decided to stay for a drink or two. Depending on who's at the bar when I get off, dictates my length of stay. The kid was still there, and more men came and filled the bar. Every time I'd look in his direction, he'd look the other way or pretend he didn't notice I was looking. I chatted with a few regulars and eventually went out back. There were a couple of men messing around, but nothing too serious.

A silver haired man in a business suit stood next to me. Before I knew it, I felt his hand on my crotch. I was horny anyway, so I let him feel and take my cock out. He wasted no time getting on his knees and stuffing my cock down his throat. It felt good, and as I held his gray head, trying to stuff my cock down his gullet, I felt myself being watched. I looked up and in the dim light I saw the kid with the brow ring watching. He stood some distance away, not wanting to intrude. As soon as he realized that I knew he was watching, he turned away. I wanted him to watch. Sometimes I can be a bit of an exhibitionist. I was disappointed when he left, but continued to enjoy the silver haired man's mouth and throat. Again the kid came to watch, this time a little closer. I was really enjoying the kid watching and made an effort to adjust my position allowing him a better view. Then again, he left.

"Fuck!" I thought. So I patted my silver haired daddy on the head and told him I wanted to take a break. He reluctantly gave up his post and I headed back into the bar. The kid was again playing pinball, and then eventually came close to where I was standing, but didn't speak.

"Hi," I said. "Nice brow ring." He looked at me, said hello, and told me his name was Danny. I guess he didn't know what else to say to me because he suddenly went back outside.

"Shit!" I said to myself. "Why do they make it so difficult?" I wasn't going to let him get away and followed him. I found him standing in the exact spot where I was getting sucked minutes before. I went over and stood next to him.

"So?" I asked, letting the question hang in the night air. He looked at me, but said nothing. This was getting to be a bore. He was making me do all the work. So I got bold and reached out my hand to touch his crotch and was surprised to find that his fly was already open. I reached inside his baggy boxers. Then I turned my cap backwards, positioned myself in front of him, and got down on my knees, ready to service the boy. I dug out his flaccid cock.

"You gonna blow me?" he finally asked in his manly voice.

"Yeah, that's the idea!" I told him and brought his cock to my mouth. He was circumcised, and he had a fresh, clean scent as if he had just showered before coming here.

Inside my expert mouth his young cock started to swell. I sucked, trying my best to give him pleasure. His cock grew in response. To my surprise, it grew and grew and grew. Before long my mouth was filled with a bigger than average fat cock. It was almost too big to fit the whole thing into my mouth. Almost inaudibly I heard him telling me to suck him.

"Oh yeah, suck it, dude. You know how to suck." I felt the head of his cock against the back of my throat while his hand behind my head forced it down into my throat.

"Oh yeah, I love that," he groaned. I know from experience how much men love having their cocks down another man's throat and feeling the head against the back of it.

I was enjoying this too. I leaned back, taking his cock out to get a better look at it. I couldn't believe how big it was. It was slick with my spit. Its head was wide and the shaft had veins running along the length of it.

"Oh don't stop, dude! It's hard to find anyone who can do it like you're doing. Come on, do it to me."

I smiled to myself and resumed my sucking while inspecting his body. I wondered to myself why this baggy look was such a big fashion. It really hid his body. His flat belly was taut and smooth, barely a hair on it, only a line of fine hair from his belly button to his cock.

As I was sucking, someone came over and tried to put his hand between my mouth and his cock. The boy quickly pushed the hand away.

"Don't dude," he snapped. "He knows what he's doing." I really liked this kid's attitude, forceful, and he knew what he wanted.

I slid my mouth back onto his cock and again it filled my mouth. I couldn't help the amount of spit and it dripped down my beard, coating it and my hand. At times I would use my hand along with my mouth, running it along the thick shaft.

He opened his shirt despite the fact that it was cold. Luckily, back here we were protected from the rain and wind by the large fence and canopy. With one hand he played with his left nipple, the other he held firmly behind my head, pulling me to him. It was getting difficult to keep up with his thrusts, as my jaws started to ache.

"Take it, dude! Take it down!" he pleaded. "Oh yeah, suck me!" He was trying to shove his fat cock down my gullet, grinding his crotch against my face, making my eyes water, but I held on. He held me there for a moment then let me slide my mouth along his shaft again. At the same time I had my own cock out and was jacking it as I sucked. I was working overtime on this kid, and loving every minute, not to mention every inch.

"Oh yeah, dude, here it comes!" he announced. I felt his cock swelled even larger, as the head throbbed, spurting forth its syrupy nectar. I fought to keep up, as spit mixed with cum dripped from the corner of my mouth. Finally, his cock began to soften as he let go of my head.

"Thanks, dude!" he said as he lifted his pants and buttoned his shirt. "I needed that. You're the best!" he patted my head and left.

I hadn't realized it, but we had attracted a small group of onlookers. All were jacking themselves or each other. I stood and two bears came close and planted their mouths on my tits. The silver haired man came back and resumed sucking my cock. A tall handsome man leaned over and kissed my mouth, tasting the remains of the boy's cum. I think most if not all of us shot, each moaning and thrashing. Yeah it was just another boring day on the job.

~

MOUNTAIN MEN

On a drizzly afternoon in late April, 1841, James Jeremiah Foster rode into town, tired and dirty from his long journey. Better known as Mountain Man Jim, he was glad to finally get into town. The rutted streets of Fort Laramie were rivers of mud this time of year, but still busy with immigrants and traders making ready their wagons and outfits for the journey to Oregon or California. The hotels were crowded, and the gunsmiths and saddlers were kept constantly at work providing arms and equipment for the different groups of travelers.

Mountain Man Jim stood six feet-three inches tall, rawboned, with a power build. His eyes were pale gray like a cool, winter morning and his full head of brown hair was tied back, lying neatly against his neck. His beard, speckled with gray, hadn't seen a razor in many years. Folks said he was a companionable man with a remarkable sense of humor.

He loved to shock the greenhorns from the old states with his tall tales. He would tell of Glass Mountains, "peetrified" birds singing "peetrified" songs, and reminisce about the days when Pike's Peak was just a hole in the ground. Of course, all these accounts were told in absolute seriousness so that he was able to fool pert near everyone. Then he'd laugh and say he was only joshing.

He held onto the reigns of his horse, Old Blue, as his sharp eyes ranged down the streets, taking in everything at once. Following close behind was Montgomery, his pack mule loaded down with a harvest of pelts. The winter had been long and hard, not to mention lonely. But after years of solitary living, a body got used to it. Even so, a wild man would crave the company of humans, and sometimes, the smell or touch of a man. It wasn't that he didn't have humans to talk to, but they were usually the local Indians, and sometimes he just didn't want to work at communicating in sign language or one of the Indian dialects. And it wasn't that he didn't like Indians either; on the contrary, he was blood-brother to a Shoshone brave and adopted member of the tribe. But on the advent of spring he always got the craving for the company of white men. He was anxious to talk, and the Green River Rendezvous was now a thing of the past.

His buckskins had the well-worn sheen of sweat and blood that helped make them waterproof. His fur hat, made from pine-martin skin, sat atop his head snug and secure. In his belt was a brace of faithful pistols and a huge Arkansas toothpick, or bowie knife, in a leather sheath. He'd been on the trail for weeks now and the one thing he wanted most was a hot bath, a luxury he'd only have about once a year. But first, he'd stop in at the trading post.

The trading post was at the center of town, run by proprietor Bill Sublette, a mountain man and trapper gone "entrepreneur." The former trapper was always glad to see the grizzly ol' mountain man and even looked forward to his visits. They were old friends and had a special bond from hunting and trapping together years before.

Jim walked in with a burden of skins slung over one shoulder and unloaded them onto the wooden counter. "Not in all your born days will you believe how I come by these'n ere, skins," he stated.

"Howdy, Jim," Bill said. "What fool story you gonna' give me this year?" The store was full of immigrants, traders, and Indians, all looking curiously at the grizzly mountain man.

"No story Bill," he said. "Nothin' but the dag-burn truth." The older trader looked at Mountain Man Jim, wondering what sensational story would be told. Jim dug into a pouch at his side and pulled out a carved bone pipe and a tobacco pouch. Slowly, he filled the pipe and lit it, purposely setting the tension. Everyone waited for him to begin his story.

"Well sir," he said finally, "I 'as hunting up the old north trace one day with not much luck. It was one of 'em strange twilight times in the full moon of mid-winter and it was dad burn cold, so cold that had I lit a fire, it woulda' froze solid.

Snow had come down and it was quiet as the grave. I'd jest 'bout given up 'n the day 'as growing dark when I come across an assemblage. It was the most peculiar rendezvous I'd ever laid eyes on. At first I thought they 'as an Injun hunting party, but as I got closer, I seed they wasn't men at all, Injun or otherwise; they 'as critters!" he emphasized.

"They musta' heard the crunch of the snow under my feet, 'cause they all looked to me as I come up. The leader of this peculiar band o' mangy critters was this ol' bar that musta' been fifteen feet high on two feet and white as new fallen snow. The crowd of varmints parted, and he come up to me on all fours, his big body swayin' to and fro, and then looked me straight in the eye, took a big sniff at me, and pert near sucked my whiskers off my face."

Everyone, including Bill looked on in amazement.

"With that big varmint so close I thought he 'as gonna swaller me up in a single bite, I slowly reached into my pouch and took a handful of tobacco and brought it up to my mouth. He didn't know what tobacco was, and he was curious so he smelled it right up into his snout. He commenced to wheezin' and coughin' that he finally keeled over – dead." he stopped and drew on his pipe.

"Then what happened?" said an emigrant.

"The rest of 'em knew I 'as huntin' and in need of some skins," he continued while gesturing with the end of his pipe.

"I could see they 'as powerful hungry and they 'as meanin' to eat me right then and thar." He stopped and took a long, slow draw off his pipe.

"Luckily," he continued. "I had me some buffalo jerky I cured the summer afore, and I said I'd give it to 'em if'n they'd let me be. Well, they took a gander at that ol' barr lying there dead and then at me, thinking I had some powerful magic. They was so full of gratitude that I didn't kilt 'em too that they stood up on their hind legs, like they 'as men, took off their pelts and handed 'em right over to me."

Bill just stood there not saying a word, his mouth frozen open. Others gathered round to hear the tale too, all mesmerized.

"You ol' mountain goat," Bill said finally. "If'n that's the truth, I'll eat that mangy hat of yours."

"Well, Billy, you best start eatin,' cause that's the honest-to-God-truth."

Everyone looked from the old proprietor then to Big Jim and back. No one said a word.

"Well then, whar's the white pelt you got off that big barr?" Jim looked up and slowly a smile emerged from his white speckled whiskers.

"Ok Billy, you got me," he confessed. "Jist keepin' you on your toes – don't want 'em green horns gittin' the better side o' you."

"I knows how to keep 'em from gittin' the better a' me. Don't you be worryin' yehself none bout that," the store keeper said.

"Yup, that's rightly true, we been round a long time," Jim agreed. "Wasn't long ago you and me was trappin' together, though."

"Them was the days; we could walk around naked as savages for hundreds of miles and never see a soul, least not a white one," Bill added.

"For you know it, these settlers will be livin' on top of us," Jim complained. "Gittin' so I got to watch where I step or I might trip over one."

"Ain't that the truth, every Spring more come through 'ere on their way to Oregon or Californy. The trail is a place to trade, you know that? You might think a openin' up such a place. You ain't gittin' any younger."

"Yup, I knows that. You keep tellin' me that year after year, too. 'Asides, I been thinkin' along 'em lines. Don't be surprised when I come to be your competition. Anyways, you look these skins over and give me a fair price. Right now I'm hankerin' for a bath more 'an anythin.'" Jim said scratching his beard and squinting one eye. "The saloon still got that place out back a thar that has 'em tubs?"

"Yup, they do, but a new place opened up since you 'as here last. A Chinese feller by the name of Lu Chin got a place jest pass Sadie's that's a whole lot better. 'Em Chinese are good, hard workers, and clean too, so clean you kin jest 'bout eat off 'em," Bill said.

The more Jim thought about a hot bath, the itchier he got. He was going to do just one more thing first. He got Bill to advance him a few coins and he set off.

"I'll leave old Blue and Montgomery here," he said then wished Bill a good day and set off.

The big mountain man headed for the other side of town and the only saloon. He looked around and shook his head. *"Humanity is gittin' closer and closer,"* he thought.

At the saloon, aptly name "The Saloon," there were Indians milling inside and out, some in old blankets, others drinking too much, their half-wild ponies tied close by. Inside he walked up to the bar and ordered a whiskey. The place was large and cool, full of men, noise and smoke. In one corner a happy faced Negro played an upright piano. The professional women that inhabited the place were laughing and giggling, each trying to outdo the other. Most of the men were just as dirty and smelly as he was. There were a few exceptions, fancy men from the old states, smoking their fine cigars and sipping high priced whiskey. He always found these "dandies" amusing and even entertained a few in his life, but he just wanted to drink a few and get a bath. He looked around, there wasn't a Mormon's chance in hell he was gonna' see anyone he knew, not with all these immigrants around. He was about to drink down his whiskey and leave when someone held his arm.

"You weren't thinking about leaving, were you sir?" Jim turned and looked down into two intense sky-blue eyes, under which a thick handle bar moustache was well trimmed and waxed to fine points. The man was well dressed but nowhere near as tall as Jim and the fine city suit did little to conceal his powerful frame.

"Actually I was, sir," Jim replied. "Gotta get this ol' body clean."

"I was about to offer you a drink in return for a story," the man said, smiling with a cigar clenched between white teeth. "I hear all you big trappers have stories to tell about Indians and such."

Jim couldn't resist telling a story and getting a free drink at the same time, but he couldn't help feeling somewhat intimidated standing next to this well-dressed, clean man.

"Well, sir," he said "I'd like nothin' better, but all I want now is a hot bath."

"Sir, one drink won't make you any dirtier than you are now. None of these men care how dirty you are. For that matter, neither do I," he added, then smiled. "Maybe on your way back, but please take this whiskey in advance." Jim thanked the man then guzzled down his whiskey, winked at him and walked out.

Back outside the sounds of the saloon faded once again into noises of hooves in mud and the clinking and clattering of wagons on the move. Men barked and women scolded while young ones ran along the wooden walks, yipping and yapping, like coyote pups. Jim felt the warmth of the whiskey start to fill his belly. A great pressure released off his back and was replaced by one in his crotch. He was anxious to see this new bathhouse and there was scarcely nothing better than a private session of self-pleasure in hot, relaxing bath water.

He continued on his way then turned the corner and there was Sadie's, Fort Laramie's most popular whorehouse. On its balcony were half-dressed women, displaying themselves and waving white lace hankies.

"Come on up, mountain man," said a brassy redhead. "I got something you can climb." She had large breasts that barely seemed able to fit inside her corset.

"You sure a big 'n too!" said another. "I bet you got somethin' big to skin for me."

Jim felt his face grow red.

"Maybe after I make myself more presentable, I might," he yelled up. "But not likely," he said under his breath.

Lu Chin's was next door; just as ordinary and nondescript as all the buildings in town, only it was newer. A small sign over the door read: "Baths five cents." Inside it was dark and warm, a somewhat sweet smelling odor hung on the air, almost suffocating him. Behind the counter at one end of the room was an older Chinese gentleman, who momentarily looked up, nodded then continued to scribble into a ledger. The wall behind him was covered in some kind of richly decorated cloth.

"Howdy," Jim said. The Chinaman looked up and smiled.

"Yes?"

"I'm here to use your facilities," Jim said.

"Yes?" the Chinaman repeated.

"Do you speak English?"

"Yes," he replied.

"Ah very well, I would like to use your facilities."

"Yes," he said again.

Jim looked at the old man for while. "How much will that be?"

"Yes," he repeated again.

"Dag-burn it!" Jim cussed. "Who you got t' FUCK to git any service 'round here?"

Suddenly the old man's face lit up.

"No fuck. No fuck here. Next dor, next dor. Plenty fuck next dor."

"No, I don't want to fuck. I want a bath! A b-a-a-t-t-h!" he said dragging out the word and waving his hands in front as if he was swimming. The old Chinaman just looked at him like he was crazy and scratched his head.

"'Scuze me," a voice came from behind them. Jim turned to see the broad shouldered city fellow he met at the saloon moving towards the counter.

"Allow me." he said to Jim then turned to the Chinaman and started talking to him in a funny language Jim didn't understand. The Old Chinaman smiled and started talking rapidly in the curious lingo. Jim was surprised listening to them talk and hearing the strange words coming from the city fellow's mouth was something he didn't expect. He knew English, French, and a few Indian dialects, even sign language, but this one was one he didn't know, and it was hard on the ears. Like bits of metal hitting against each other.

Finally the city fellow turned around.

"It's this way," he said to Jim while handing him a rough towel.

"But the cost?" Jim asked.

"You can buy me a drink after." Then he showed Jim through a cloth draped door behind the counter.

It was hot in the back and steamy. Jim noticed a few men in wooden tubs. The far wall had pegs for your clothes. Here and there were wooden benches. In the center of the room was a huge iron cast stove with buckets and pans of water heating. Some of the tubs were situated in stalls or nooks with a wool curtain hanging on rope for privacy. In the rough-sawn wood floor were ruts or troughs in line with the tubs for letting out the water.

The city fellow led them to one of the small alcoves that had two tubs side by side.

"Here's a couple that are out of the way," the feller said. Jim looked at him.

"That's mighty neighborly friend, but I was hoping for some privacy."

"Kit, call me Kit. Everyone does."

"Well Mr. Kit," Jim began.

"Just Kit," the shorter and younger man interrupted.

"Ok, Kit, I'm much obliged, but I really do need my own space."

"You can't say no," Kit said as he started to take his clothes off. "The deed's done and already paid for, so you might as well take your skins off and enjoy it." Jim finally gave up and decided that he might as well.

"Now, I don't want to offend you, sir."

"Kit!" the younger man corrected.

"But I haven' washed in weeks." Kit stopped just as he was about to unbutton his trousers.

"Is that what's bothering you. I've been with men who've been dirtier than you, even been dirtier myself."

"Suit yaself, but ya' been warned."

They both continued to undress in silence. As Jim was turning round he noticed Kit's backside. It was a powerful muscular butt, round and firm, just what you'd expect on stout man of his size. He notice one other thing, just above and off to the side, was a deep scar.

"Looks like a tomahawk's work," Jim thought.

"Whar did a city feller like you get that?"

Kit turned around trying to see what Jim was talking about.

"What? Where?"

"Jest above your ass," he said touching it lightly. "Right thar!" Kit was half turned around sticking his ass out slightly.

"That 'n 'er!" Jim added.

"Oh that, just an old fighting scar. I'd forgotten 'bout that along ago." The younger man turned to face his larger opponent. Mountain Man Jim looked down slightly to the shorter Kit. "Looks like you got a few stories to tell also," he said pointing out a few scars on Jim's arms and chest. Kit let his hand linger, just to test the big trapper. Jim involuntarily closed his eyes and marveled at the other man's touch.

Kit was naked now, but Jim still had his leggings on. It'd been awhile since he felt another man's touch.

"Them are some muscles," Kit said running his hand across Jim's hairy chest. Within the fur-like hair he felt some scars.

"How'd these happen?"

"Oh, ya know things hap'n when ya're out trappin'" Jim's voice was quieter now, dreamy. Suddenly a noise from across the room brought them back to reality. It was a porter, a black youngster, bringing hot water to their tubs.

"Pardon me, suhs. Mr. Chin thoughts you might be needin' moe hot wata."

"Thank you son, jest make sure thar's plenty of hot water fer both of us."

"Yes, suh!" the boy said then disappeared. Jim sat and continued to take off his skins. They were wet, and in this bathhouse Jim noticed how dreadful they smelled.

"Ooooeee! Thank the Creator a skunk can't smell his own hole, otherwise he'd never mate."

"But if he couldn't smell himself or others, how could he find his own kind," Kit added, smiling, then started to get into the tub, one leg at a time. Jim noticed the dark hairy furrow of Kit's muscular ass and the way his nut sack hung low. He allowed himself to stare, not in the least bit ashamed. He liked looking at this man's body, it was compact and powerful; most of all he was hairy. Kit stood there a while, splashing hot water up onto his hairy belly and chest.

"I don't think you smell so bad," he told Jim. The water dripped over and off his cock with its head just showing from under the protecting skin. Then he let out his breath with a whoosh of air as he settled into the warm water

"Ahhh, that's nice," he cooed.

Jim finally stood up and undid the ties to his leggings and let them fall. He liked being naked – wasn't easy in the cities. Then he lifted one leg after the other as he got into the other tub. He knew Kit was watching, and it did make him a little self-conscious but he liked the thought of the other man admiring his back side. He stood there while he undid his hair, letting it fall over his shoulders. After adjusting himself to the water, he turned.

"So, why'd ya decide on comin' here?" he asked Kit.

"I come through town a few times a year."

"No, I was meanin' to this 'ere bathhouse?" he said as he brought water over his head. "Ya look mighty clean already."

"You mentioned needing a bath, so I figured I'd come too and soak a while. Makes a man feel good and relaxed," he said as he reached over and took a cigar out of his pack and lit it. He took a long, deep draw and let out a billow of smoke as he watched Jim soaping up his hair. He turned again, and this time, fished out a bottle.

"This 'ere is the finest Kentucky whiskey this side of the Rockies," he stated. He bit off the cork and lifted the bottle to Jim in salutation then drank deeply.

"Ooooie! That's nice," he said then handed it over to the older man.

Like most of his fellow mountain men, Jim loved to drink. You weren't a full-fledged mountain man unless you drank with the best of them. He took the bottle and drank deeply too.

"Mighty fine, mighty fine," he repeated while looking at the bottle. They sat awhile, smoking and enjoying the warm water, while around them the low murmur of men talking drifted across the room, when Jim noticed a peculiar sound. Out of habit he strained his ears to listen and identify the sound.

"I hear it too," said Kit.

Each sat quiet, one ear pointing skyward, listening and wondering.

"What'n ya suppose that is?" Jim asked. Kit was first to guess then Jim as they turned and smiled to each other.

"Well I'll be, you know what that is?" Kit whispered. His eyes were lit up now glowing like a child's on Christmas morning.

"Someone's doin' someone else a favor." Jim screwed up one eye, listened and smiled too. "The Shoshone's say it's the call that'll bring out the wild in men, reaches deep down inside and pulls at yer balls."

"Must be in the next stall," Kit said. "Yeah, I can see movement through that knot hole." Jim looked and saw it about three feet off the floor, squinted one eye and tried to peer though. Kit was closer and could see clearer.

"Sure enough," he said, "looks like something going on in there."

"Best to let 'em be," Jim said as he held onto Kit's arm. "No sense'n interruptin' a man's privacy."

"If a man wanted privacy, he wouldn't be doing such things in a public place. Besides, I think he's not alone." Then he scooted out of his tub with the grace of a cat, squatted down next to the knot hole and peered through.

"Damn!" he hissed. "Jim you've got see this."

"Best not," Jim said merely sitting there, not wanting to intrude. Then after a short time, he added, "What's goin' on in thar anyway?"

"There's a varmint on his knees at a knot hole on the other wall and it looks like some other fella's got his cock through, son of a coyote bitch, and the cock chafer is sucking on it!"

Jim, not able to stand it any longer, finally got out of the tub then stood next to Kit who was still kneeling. The younger man looked from the knot hole up to Jim.

"You've got to see this," he said. Jim squatted down, too, and peered through the hole. In the other stall was a long, blond haired man he didn't recognize, dressed only in worn long johns.

The man was relentlessly bobbing his head back and forth onto a cock that was jutting through the other hole. There was something in the man's manner that Jim could tell he was another city fellow. Every so often the man would stop and grind his head onto the cock he was working on. From the looks of things, it was obvious that the man was enjoying what he was doing. Also obvious, was that he didn't care who was watching.

Jim continued to watch along side of Kit, their faces side by side.

"Damn," Jim said. "That varmint sure knows how t' please a man." Then he looked to Kit who was looking back.

"Don't look hard to me," Kit said. "Besides, there ain't no harm in doing a partner a favor, right? I mean we all do it, when you ain't got women around."

"Yup, wouldn't be the first time," Jim admitted. Suddenly the man on the other side was at the knot hole too; peering back. Instinctively, they pulled their heads back as the man lightly ran a finger through.

"Come on!" he whispered. "Pass it on through and give it here!" Jim knew what the man wanted just as well as Kit did. But before either of them could answer, the man was gone; unable to wait. Another man, either trapper or immigrant had entered the man's stall and was about to give him what he wanted.

Jim and Kit stood up together, each seeing the excitement in the other. Jim towered over Kit's sturdy, hairy body, his cock lengthening with every pulse of blood running through him.

"Damn! That makes a man hot." Kit said while studying the big mountain man's cock and licking his lips. "I'm not sure that fella could have taken all this," he said as he ran his fingers lightly over the sensitive skin of Jim's lengthening cock. Jim could only suck in his breath and looked up while closing his eyes.

"You neither," he added.

Together they stood there with their cock heads almost touching.

"I've got to' see what's going on in there," Kit said anxiously and bent down to see, while Jim remained standing. "Damn, now the varmint's getting' corn holed," he whispered then looked up at Jim, his cock hanging so close. The mountain man's scent hung in the closed in stall; it was strong and musky.

Then, without shame, Kit snaked out his tongue, just barely touching the tip of Jim's cock. He looked up to see the big mountain man, backed off a bit and only a thin spider web of spit connected them. Jim sucked in his breath as he felt Kit's hot breath on his cock, then his hand wrap around its girth. And before he knew it, Kit slid back the protective skin and inhaled the head into his hot mouth.

"Damn!" Jim hissed. He had to steady himself against the wall as he felt like he was about to fall.

Kit slowly slid his hot, wet mouth over Jim's cock, then back off, each time he marveled at its size. He was right about this mountain man; he was big. Kit held the cock tight against the base as he studied it; it was fat, bloated, and shiny with spit. He started up again, taking the wild mountain cock down to its base then he'd pull back almost all the way off the hooded mushroom head. He was in full motion now, giving him absolute pleasure. Spit was frothing at the corners of Kit's mouth and dripping down his chest. At the same time Kit's other hand was under Jim's balls, pulling them along with the whole cock. Jim held onto Kit's head, his fingers dug into the long hair, as he tried to hold it still. He was fucking Kit's mouth; that hot, wet pussy mouth. Until finally,

"Stop, stop," Jim gasped, pushing Kit's face away.

He collapsed against the wooden wall holding his chest as if he was having an attack.

"Sakes alive, boy, let me catch m' breath."

"What's wrong?" Kit asked, "Don't you like it?"

"'Course I liked it. Didn't I look like I liked it? Been too long since I had that done to me, and I don't want to waste that feelin.'" He pulled Kit up to his feet and wrapped his arms around Kit's wide, hairy shoulders. "Damn! Ya're good!"

"Why'd you want me to stop then?"

"I've spent the whole of last winter with only my horse and mule for company, and outside of an Injun huntin' party now and then; it's been a while since I felt that magic down there. 'Asides, it's happenin' too fast," he complained. "I don't want to cap a climax jest yet." He looked down into Kit's eyes; they were as blue as the sky over the Rockies in summer, then he bent down and kissed Kit tenderly. Kit responded by offering his tongue. They moaned in unison and pressed themselves into each other, their wet chest hair mingling and meshing together.

Kit liked having this big man's arms around him. He'd been watching the mountain man for some time in the saloon and now he couldn't believe he had been right about him. Kit was the first to let go and lowered his face to Jim's chest, first kissing then licking his nipples. Then he did something Jim never felt another man do to him; Kit started using his teeth.

"Oh, Lord!" Jim hissed as Kit bit down harder. The shorter man held onto Jim's cock, stroking the ample foreskin back and forth slowly; the slick wet sounds filled the intimate space. Jim pressed Kit's head against his chest; the feeling was intense and the pain just barely tolerable, but he was enjoying it. He liked the way Kit used his mouth and teeth, like a wolf cub nursing and biting at the same time. Jim pulled at the hair on Kit's back and shoulders. It was one thing he missed when with Indian men; most were muscular but smooth.

In his excited state, Jim was aware of only a few things; his breathing and Kit's incessant licking. The feeling of his cock being milked was almost too much for him, he felt himself about to let go. Every time Kit bit down he felt it coming closer and closer. It had been a while since he climaxed with another man, and he didn't want to waste it by letting it spill onto the ground.

Kit could tell the big mountain man was about to let go, but he wanted to get into a better position. There was so much more he wanted to do. Their minds were on one thing and they didn't want to lose this connection. Somehow Kit maneuvered the big man closer to the tubs, and with Jim drunk with pleasure, got him into the larger one. Without Jim realizing it, Kit got in too, straddling one thick leg over the big, furry mountain man.

"Let me wash your chest," he said. Jim was half submerged and the hot, soothing water not to mention the whiskey he had drunk made him feel drowsy. Kit sat atop Jim's belly soaping his hairy chest. Thick swirls of rich lather and black hair entangled Kit's fingers. Every so often he'd tease and pinch Jim's hard nipples. At the same time he leaned forward to kiss Jim.

Jim felt as though he was asleep and this was all a dream; it felt warm and soothing and he responded to Kit's mouth with passion. Their bodies meshed together, chest to chest, belly to belly and ass to cock. Jim's unbending cock stood up like a beacon along the furrow of Kit's hairy ass while the scent of the rich soap and their man musk filled the little alcove. Kit reached back and maneuvered Jim's cock closer to his ass opening. The wild cock oozed pre-cum with every stroke as Kit's swabbed it against his pucker-hole. The egg white-like liquid was warm and slimy, making it easy to slip in.

"Mmmmm," he moaned into Jim's mouth. Jim sucked in his breath in surprise.

"No," he gasped.

"Yes. Yes, please," Kit begged.

But Jim couldn't resist. The warm, corn silk softness of Kit's inner ass was more than he could bear. He wanted this and he wanted it bad. He pressed forward slowly lifting Kit almost out of the water.

"Ahhhhh!" Kit sighed as he felt Jim's cock slide in. All the while their mouths and tongues meshed together, not willing to part. Jim's large, calloused hands held Kit's hips in place as he continued to push and started the age-old rhythm. Kit could feel Jim's cock split his ass apart and penetrate deeper and deeper into his bowels as it wormed its way inside. He loved this feeling of being filled with the uncivilized mountain man's wild cock. Jim's cries of, "Oh, Lord," were muffled against Kit's wet, trembling lips.

"Come on, you mountain devil, fuck me. Fuck my hairy ass!"

Jim looked up and searched Kit's blue eyes. His face was wet and his once waxed handle-bar moustache drooped over the sides of his chin. His long hair hung over his face in moist tangles. He continued to thrust up into Kit's muscular ass as he watched his face, looking for signs of discomfort or distress. His cock, once a liability with women, was something to be envied among men. But he also knew from past experiences that he could hurt a man if he wasn't careful or wasn't gentle. He learned to distinguish between the looks of pleasure or pain. Kit's face was a mixture of both.

Kit looked down into Jim's dark, wild face, hard with lines and sun wrinkled. His long beard, speckled with gray, floated in the water and mingled with his chest hair. He'd seen this man so many times, so many places. He wasn't handsome, per se, but he was appealing in a rugged, masculine way. Kit couldn't believe he was actually here. It was like a dream, a fantasy he had so many times. Now here he was with Mountain Man Jim; a man he admired and wanted for so long.

Jim closed his eyes tight in complete concentration, pushing and thrusting. He was close now and couldn't hold back. It'd been a long time since he'd done anything like this, and it wasn't going to take much to put him over. The feeling of his cock being milked by Kit's muscular ass was too intense.

"Kit, I'm gonna..." he said without finishing.

"Yeah!" Kit agreed, throwing his head back, his wet hair flew and landed with a splat on his back sending rivulets of water high into the air. Jim gave one last thrust and lifted Kit high. He pushed, and at the same time pulled Kit to him, impaling him firmly onto his exploding cock. Kit arched his back and gasped like he'd been punched in the belly as he felt Jim climax inside him and assault his prostate. Then without touching himself, he capped his own climax.

"Arrrgh," he groaned. It flew high and landed on Jim's chest and face, not once but twice. Slowly, Jim regained his breath as he relaxed and lowered his body. Kit bent forward and planted a kiss on his lips. Sensuously, he licked Jim's face clean. The big man responded by opening his mouth and kissing back. Kit started to get up and out, but Jim held him.

"No, not yet, stay there a minute," Kit relaxed and snuggled back into Jim's arms.

"How different this big wild mountain man is," Kit thought. Most men like Jim couldn't wait to part after. Maybe it was the feeling of their shattered sexuality that made them want to part so soon after?

Together they stayed that way for some time, not saying anything with Jim kissing the top of Kit's head until the water cooled.

After they got out, they dried each other intimately, like two old friends after a day's work. Jim had the foresight to bring along an extra pair of skins. A mountain man never traveled far without a dry set of clothes. Out in the wilderness it could mean life or death. He brought them out of his backpack and laid them neatly side by side. They were exquisitely sewn and embroidered with rich Shoshone quillwork and symbols. Kit watched as Jim groomed himself with as much care and purpose as a statesman might have. His hair was attended to and combed out, then tied back neatly behind his head; one loose strand hung to the side, entwined with a crow feather and a brightly colored bead. The clean leggings were snug and hung perfectly on his large frame. And Kit couldn't help noticing the cod piece did little to hide what lay underneath. His footwear was a combination of boot and moccasin, stuffed with deer hair to help keep them warm and dry.

Kit had a clean set of clothes of his own, only it wasn't a city suit; they were a set of skins like Jim's, but not as fancy. And unlike his city attire, they were comfortably worn and clean. His long hair, like Jim's, was attended to with much care. The last bit of detail was his moustache; he brought out a tin of wax and fixed it to sharp points once again.

Once they were fully clothed they looked at each other and smiled.

"I kinda' thought you weren't as city as you looked," Jim said. "You got some wild in you after all."

"Yeah, and I was thinking you'd wash up pretty good," Kit added.

"How 'bout you and me get us some grub and do this town up right?" Jim asked.

"Sure, and I got a room at the hotel. You can stay after, if you'd like," Kit offered. "Besides, you owe me a story."

Together, they picked up their bags and headed out of Lu Chin's. Outside the afternoon had melted into twilight and the drizzle had stopped. Just over the mountains, the full moon shone brightly. The mountain man looked up and laid his arm on Kit's shoulder.

"Did I ever tell you the story of The Man that Fell in Love with the Moon?" They left Lu Chin's together, two mountain men, two close friends out on the town. Ready for anything that might come their way.

~

THE MANHANDLER SALOON

I drove north on Halsted Street, towards one of my favorite bars; a Levi and leather bar called the Manhandler Saloon. It's on Halsted St. but far south of the gay area known as "Boy's Town."

The bar is a quiet, dark place. It's small and fills easily. You seldom hear the cackle of wispy voices you do in other trendy bars. Not that it's unfriendly. On the contrary, the place is very friendly. What they call "user friendly." There's always someone there to "give you a hand" or take your mind off your troubles. Country music is usually playing, as most of the good bartenders are sorta' country anyway, but you can find all types there, from generation X to biker types and just about everything in between. I'd say it's one of Chicago's best kept secrets.

Seeing the owner standing at his usual place at the bar, I ordered a beer and walked toward him. He's a bear type, with thick graying hair, cut into a flat top. I've known him for years, and you can usually find me there talking with him. In the last year since I split-up with my lover-partner, we've become really good friends. We both lost our partners. Only he lost his to death. Mine just got stupid.

We were having a good ol' time discussing one of the bartender's dicks, which is supposed to be a handful, when I noticed a tall kid standing at the service bar. I say a kid, but I knew he had to be at least twenty-one to even get into any bar. He just looked so young. The boy was tall, as I said, maybe six feet with longish red hair. After carding him, Brian, the bartender studied the ID, then brought it over to the owner and asked if it was ok. He gave it a quick look and handed it back to the bartender.

"Yeah, give the boy a drink," he said in his Texas drawl. The boy nodded in our direction, took his drink then disappeared into the crowd. I looked, trying to see where he'd gone.

"Nick, you've got that look again," the owner said.

"What look?" I asked trying to appear nonchalant.

"That look that means trouble," he said with a gleam in his eye. "Besides, I thought you only liked Daddy types?"

"You mean like you?" I said smiling. He put his arm around me and looked at me close.

"Well, if you don't go after it, I will," he said as he tugged playfully at my salt and pepper colored beard. "My, that's getting long," he said, pulling me closer and kissing me passionately.

"Hey! Stop that!" the bartender yelled. "Am I gonna have to turn the hose on you guys?"

"Yeah, maybe I'll go out to the 'Back 40' and just see what's happening." I said to him.

The Back 40 is an area just beyond the patio. It's fenced in by an eight foot tall privacy fence that was put up for security. Now it's a great hangout for action. It's dark and very private.

I walked out back, saying my howdy's and hello's to some of the regulars. At night, the Back 40 is bathed in deep shadows. The only light is what filters in from the alley and street lamps, so it takes a few seconds to get used to the darkness.

Soon I spotted the boy. He stood with his back to the fence farthest away from me. I started to walk in his direction, when someone stepped in front of him and began talking to him. Well, it seemed as though this was not going to be one of my nights.

"Oh well, maybe next time." I thought. I returned to the front bar and resumed my position with the owner.

"That was quick," he said without looking at me.

"He was busy," I answered. The subject was dropped.

Life went on and I soon forgot about the boy. We had been standing there chit-chatting, when I happened to turn around and saw the boy sitting on a stool opposite us by himself. I tipped my hat and he nodded. He was very cute – too cute to be by himself. Almost everyone around him was trying to attract his attention. I smiled to myself, thinking how it was when I was his age, and turned back to my old friend; we resumed our chat.

A short time later..

"Can I buy you two handsome men a drink?" I turned around and looked up to see the boy behind me.

"Why, sure you can, son," the owner said. We ordered our drinks and thanked the boy.

"My name's Nick" I offered. We found out his name was Matthew, but preferred Matt. He mentioned he was from Texas, and that created more interest for the bar owner. I felt a little left out, as they were both from that area of the country and at least had that in common.

"I take it this is your first time here," I asked.

"Yeah, a friend of mine told me about this place, and said it was a good place to meet older guys."

"Well, you've got your pick here," I heard the owner say. Besides Dandy's or Gentry's, this is where they come. What would you like?" The kid looked at me then to the owner.

"I'd like this handsome man to kiss me," he answered, meaning me. I was extremely flattered and I'm sure I turned several shades of red.

"Well, you bought us a drink, I suppose I could at least oblige you with a kiss," I said.

He bent down to me and our lips met. We kissed for several moments and I felt myself getting aroused. Our tongues meshed as we clung to each other. I have to admit, that there is something about the first passionate kiss from a stranger that makes you want more.

"Excuse me," I heard and felt a tap at my shoulder.

"Remember me?" It was the owner. I looked at him sheepishly.

"Yeah?"

"I guess this means you're dumping me," he said smiling. It was one of his favorite sayings, along with many others.

"Am I interrupting?" Matthew asked. He looked disappointed.

"Oh no, I was just kidding. Looks like you two are hitting it off pretty good. I think I'll take a stroll out back and see if I can find someone to take pity on a poor old soul."

"Oh, brother," I said knowing full well he never had any trouble finding someone to hook up with. He always tried the passive/aggressive bullshit on me. This time I was just going to let it slip by.

"Is he pissed?" the boy asked, concerned.

"No, he just says things like that to get attention. Before long he'll be sucking some cock or in the middle of a pig pile and he'll be fine."

We talked for hours and the time went by quickly. Before we knew it, the bartenders were yelling, "Last call!"

"Shit, where'd the time go?" I asked. "I think we better be getting out of here."

"Can I give you a ride somewhere?" the kid asked.

"I was going to ask you the same question. Thanks, but I drove, too."

The look he gave me was that of a lost little boy. I knew what he wanted from me.

"You want to come over my place?" I finally asked.

"Yeah, I thought you'd never ask," the boy said excitedly.

At my apartment, he followed me in like an obedient puppy. We embraced as soon as the door was closed and hungrily pawed at each other.

"Let's take our clothes off," I suggested. He sat on the sofa while I stood before him and removed my boots and Levi's.

"You've got boxers just like my father wears," he said looking up at me.

"Does that bother you?"

"No, it's kinda' hot, really. I used to fantasize about him when I was a kid," he admitted.

"That's ok. A lot of boys fantasize about their fathers. It's only natural. You ever see your daddy's dick?" I asked him.

"Yeah," he answered shyly. "A couple of times."

I wanted to hear more, but first things first. He pulled his jeans off. His legs were long with a soft covering of copper colored down. I noticed his underwear – they were briefs. He was about to remove them.

"Keep them on a while." I said. "I want to take them off you." I kept my boxers on as well.

Taking him by the hand, I led him to the bed and he sat facing me. We kissed again.

"Oh sir," he sighed.

"It's ok, son. You're with me and safe," I said as I held him, his head against my hairy chest.

He clung to me like a small child, whimpering as he nursed on my nipple.

"Oh yes, suck Daddy's tit."

The boy felt so warm, so vulnerable. Something inside this beautiful boy needed this: this love, this embrace. He looked up at me as I held his face between my hands with those big, blue, puppy dog eyes. I realized I needed this too. *"Oh, shit!"* I thought to myself. *"I could really fall for a boy like this."* But I wasn't going to. There was no point. I knew I'd probably never see him again after tonight.

I shifted my weight and gently pushed him back onto the bed. I got on top of him, but he maneuvered himself on top of me.

"Oh, Nick!" he moaned. He lightly kissed my face, my eyes, and my nose. I was putty in his hands and couldn't believe how much I was turned on by him. He licked at my eye lids, then down my nose again, this time licking at my nostrils. I shuddered with a feeling so intense and so incredible that my breath came in gasps. He had my entire nose in his mouth and I couldn't believe the feeling.

All the while, my hands pawed at his back and notice how soft his skin was, like only a redhead can be. I moved so that I was on top and kissed his face, as he had done to me. I licked the tip of his nose. He smiled at me. My tongue flicked at his nostrils. He gasped. What a sensuous feeling. I had been tempted to do this many times, with other men, but always thought they would be repulsed. I bit at his chin, mimicking little doggy bites. He was breathing heavy now. I licked down his cheek to his neck.

"Oh, oh," he let out a whimper of a sigh. He tasted slightly salty. I bit at his neck. Not hard, I didn't want to break the skin. He cringed. I sniffed, I licked, and I bit. He was in heaven.

"Oh my God!" he gasped. "I'm so hot!" I continued down his neck to his hairless chest and swabbed his hardening nipples as I pinned his arms above his head.

"Oh, Nick!" he moaned. From his nipple, I licked from his pectoral to his armpit. I sniffed again. He was panting now. I licked at the soft hairs, pulling at them with my lips.

"Oh, sir!" he cried. I licked again then bit down.

"Argh!" he grunted and flinched at the same time. I enjoyed the taste of him, his youth, and the sharp smell of his perspiration. He wiggled and struggled. He could have gotten away, but he didn't want to. Daddy was taking him places he'd rarely been.

I continued down his left side, leaving a trail of spit as my tongue glided along his smooth skin. He twitched and gasped. I let go of his arms and felt him hold my head against his flat belly. A few wisps of fine reddish hair grew out beneath his belly button. *"An inny,"* I thought to myself as I inserted my tongue, giving him a few dog licks. I could feel his cock under my chin within the cotton material, waiting for attention. I continued down his flat belly, nibbling at the fine red hairs and at the material of his Jockey's. With both hands, I pulled them down. I traced the line of hairs with my tongue down to his pubes – they were incredibly red. I get such a thrill seeing red pubic hair.

Then as I pulled them down over his cock, it slapped up tight against his flat belly. It was longer than mine, but not quite as thick. And as most young men are, he was circumcised.

I licked from the shaft, to the head. He was already leaking ample amounts of pre-cum. With my index finger, I brushed the piss hole; a thin strand of clear fluid bridged his cock to my finger. He had a beautiful set of balls, nestled in the ball sack. They were much bigger than mine, with almost no hair. They were beautifully formed and big as hen's eggs.

I sucked his cock into my mouth, feeling the soft-hard texture.

"Oh!" he moaned. The sweet cock filled my mouth. I felt the blood pulse through his organ, throbbing. He tasted of things fresh and new. His smell was fresh, like sun-dried linen. I knew the boy had his whole life ahead of him. The feeling I was partaking in something special came to my mind. The boy was enjoying the feelings I was giving him. I slid my wet lips up and down his slick cock shaft. I used my hand as much as my mouth. My head bobbed between his outstretched legs. I knew the feelings I was giving him were almost too intense. His head was swaying from side to side.

"Oh, lord!" he said praising the gods. I swallowed his cock as far down my throat as it would go. And held it there a second. He grabbed the back of my head and grunted.

"Aumph," he said as he shoved it in deeper. "Oh, shit!" I had gone too far. I was too excited myself, and as he held my face to his crotch, his cock buried in my throat, he came.

"Oh, Nick." he cried. I felt his cock throb and swell with every spurt. The boy was cumming. My eyes watered as I fought to swallow every drop. Then he subsided and let go. Slowly, I backed my head away, the taste of his eagerness still on my tongue. One last shot landed on my moustache. The boy relaxed and lay back, his heavy breathing calmed. After a time he looked at me.

"Man that was great!" he said, pulling me up so that we were face to face. I licked at my moustache, and he did the same, tasting his own cum.

"Mmmmm," we purred in unison.

NEWT'S FIRST LESSON

It was a hot Sunday in late summer and the afternoon was dozing by like a snail in spit. High up in the oaks, a choir of cicadas was singing in harmony and the hotter it got, the louder they'd call. We'd just finished our chores and Uncle Jeb thought it a good idea to go over to the swimming hole for a cool swim. Usually we'd wash up at the horse trough but since it was so hot, he thought a dip would be more sensible-like.

Uncle Jeb was Ma's kin but young enough to be my older brother. He stood on the better part of six foot and looked to me like the biggest man in these here parts. Being that he was around my whole life, I'd seen him naked before and didn't think too much about it.

The swimming hole was on the far side of our land, just past the fence that separates the front and back forty. After we stripped off our overalls and waded in, we got to horse-playin' 'n wrasslin.' Before I knew it, he grabbed me and flung me in the water. Well o' course, I'd come back up wanting more, and I guess I brushed up too close to him one too many times 'cause his pecker got bigger and harder. Lordy, it was almighty big, and it bobbed up and down, like a tree branch in a high wind.

You shoulda' seen him standing there all tensed up with cold water up to his hairy nuts, yeah they was powerful big too, and he was hairy all over with thick, black hair, like some ol' black bear.

He was standing there breathing hard like he just pitched a bale of hay and had this strange look in his blue eyes; all possessed like. Now that I think on it, maybe he was. I'd never seen him like that before. His chest was heaving up 'n down as I was looking at him, and he asked me what I was gawking at.

"Look at your pecker," I said pointing down. "It's all swelled up." O' course I couldn't take my eyes off it.

"Gosh almighty, what made it git so big?" I asked. "You got stung by a bee or somethin?'"

He looked down to his pecker, but didn't say anything, just lifted his arms about shoulder high and pumped up his muscles.

"You wanna' feel ma' muscles, Newt?" he asked. Only he wasn't looking at me; he was studying on his muscles. I reached up and put my hand to his arm. It was so big I could scarcely fit my hand around it and it was hard like stone and his skin was cool to the touch. Suddenly, I felt funny inside, like I never did before, like I swallowed a frog. Right then 'n there, I wanted to grow up being like him.

So there he was standing in front of me, like an ol' coon dog with its pecker outta' its sheath. The water came up just under his balls, making the hairs float out along side, and his chest was heaving up 'n down right in front of my face. That's when I noticed his nipples; dark, round, 'n sticking out. Many things on God's earth have nipples, how come I'd never noticed them before was perplexing.

Without thinking, I slid my hand over his chest and felt the muscles covered with wet hair. It was matted down on him making him look darker and hairier. He looked down at me and smiled. His blue eyes were clear like an Illinois lake and gleaming like wet rocks. The hair on his head was messed up, dripping wet, and his mouth curled up under his thick moustache in a wicked smile.

"Look down boy," he tells me quiet like. I looked down and was surprised to see I was swelling up too. The head of my pecker was just sticking out from the skin like his, only I wasn't near as big. It was like setting okra next to a summer squash, he was so big. He reached down to my pecker. His hand was rough from chores, but his touch was gentle and felt good.

"Looks like that ol' bee done stung me too," I said, and then he took my hand, slid it down his chest and over his hard stomach, and left it just above his pecker. I was still looking down at it, gawking.

"How come we's so hard?" I asked.

I put my hand over his pecker and felt how hot it was, pert near pulled it right back away; it was so hot. He didn't say a word, only pulled me closer. Laying my head on his wet chest, I felt his chin whiskers and the ends of his thick moustache over my head. I could hear his heart beating fast and loud as it drummed in my ear. Then he started talking to me in a voice I'd never heard before. Like he was someone else, someone I didn't know. I wasn't afraid, just bewildered.

"Don't you know what a hard-on is, or a boner?" he asked me. "Ain't your Pa been teachin' you nothin'?"

I lifted my head and looked up into his eyes.

"Guess I don't rightly know, Uncle Jeb. Reckon he was thinkin' he'd git to that once I got older."

"Maybe so," he said and then commenced to telling me.

"A hard-on is when your pecker, or your cock, as men calls it, gits full a blood and swells up hard."

"Blood?" I asked, alarmed. "Like I was bleedin?'"

"No, not like you was bleedin,' he said to me, "but inside in your veins, comes natural. It happens sometimes when you wake up in the mornins, piss proud and you got to make water real bad. Or when you're standin' in cold water, like we's doin' now. Most times it happens when you think of sex or see some farm critters fuckin.' Makes you feel sex-like."

Then he changed the subject. "Did you clean this today?" He asks still holding my pecker.

"Yes sir," I said. "Every time I wash up."

"No, yah got to wash it proper," he told me.

"I guess so. Pa says otherwise you commence to stink and offend the women folk. But I ain't rightly sure what he meant."

"Here, let me show you." That's when he got into his teaching mode. He got that way when he commenced to explaining things. His face gets all squinty and serious and his eye brows come together like he only got one.

So he sat us down on the bank; him along side of me with his thick, hairy legs all spread out. His cock was still standing, pointing skyward, reminded me of this big ol' turtle I caught once with its head out, only prettier. Then he told me to kneel between his legs.

"Ok," he says, "wet your hands and bring some of it on my cock. Pull back the skin some, but not too far. A man's cock is powerful sensitive especially where the skin meets the head just under the piss spot. Remember that!"

"Yes sir," I said.

"See where the head flares out? Just behind it is where you got to make sure it's clean and up under on both sides of that connecting patch of skin. It builds up there during the day and gets all smelly. Some men don't like it. Personally I don't mind, long as it's not too bad. But your Pa, he never gets stinky. He's one of the nicest smelling men I've ever known. Even when he's out all day working, he comes in smelling good and strong."

Then he got all quiet like and closed his eyes. At first I thought he fell asleep. But he finally opened them again and told me to wash his nuts. I reached down and put my hand just under them. I thought to myself that they were like goose eggs, but the skin around them was velvet soft.

He told me to pull on them some, but not too hard. Seems they're powerful sensitive too. Then he said he was getting too hot and to splash more water on him. I scooped up handfuls of cool water and splashed it over his body. It spilled over his face and chest while he sucked it in. I watched as he let out air with water spurting in small droplets.

"Ok," he said. "Wash my cock again, closer this time." I returned to my place betwence his outstretched legs as he instructed me on what I needed to do next. He placed one large hand over mine, and together, we stroked his cock. Back and forth, up and down he went. I could feel it getting harder and lengthening more. It felt hard and soft all at the same time. The warm velvet- like skin slid smoothly over his cock head as it made a slushy, swishy-like sound.

"That's it boy!" he told me. "Faster."

Together we went faster with me following his lead. Then he let go and told me to finish. His hand was on his chest now, his thick fingers pinching his nipples, while his eyes glazed over as he watched me.

"Oh, fuck, Newt," he cussed. I slowed down for a second thinking I was hurting him. "No, don't stop! Keep goin,' boy. Faster!" He looked at me, all possessed like, "Yeah, oh yeah! That's it." His voice got low, like a rumble that I felt pass through my body. "Oooooh fuuuuuk." He growled and cussed like a drunken man. He told me I was a good boy and that Pa was a good man, too.

Then something unbelievable happened. He stopped for a second, pulled back his butt, and didn't move.

"Oh fuck!" he growled again. Then a thick liquid, like thin nose snot, gushed out his piss hole. It shot high in the air and landed with a splat on his chest. I let go on a cause he was having a conniption fit, and I thought he was dying, but he continued to pull on his cock as more stuff spilled out of him. A second gust shot out, hitting him square in the face, covering half his moustache. Some of it dripped off into his mouth. He didn't seem to notice. After a couple of more gushed out, the rest trickled out slower and softer then slowly he relaxed in a heap, like he was dead.

"Gosh almighty Uncle Jeb, you all right?" I asked. For a moment he just lay there not saying a word, but I could see he was still breathing.

"Yeah, let me catch my breath," he said softly. Then he sat up and splashed some water onto his face. "Damn!" He said then noticed the liquid on his hands from his face. He pulled some from his moustache and smiled at me. "Damn!" he repeated. "That don't happen too often." He got up, stretched his muscles again, and dove off the bank into deep water. He came back up sputtering air and rubbed his face, washing the strange liquid from his hair and moustache then returned to the bank beside me. I looked at him mystified.

"What happened?" I asked.

"I ejaculated," he said, smiling at me. "To put it simple, I capped a climax."

"But what about the stuff that came out?" He didn't answer, but took my hand again.

"You mean this?" He asked pointing to some of the liquid that somehow got on my hand. I stared at it, dumb like.

"That's cum, or what medical men call sperm."

"It looks like nose drippings," I said.

"Yep."

I looked at it and brought it closer to my face and smelled it. It smelled strong, but somehow familiar, like I smelled it before.

"You'll get used to it," he told me. "You might even get used to the taste," he added while twisting the end of his moustache between two fingers.

"You eat it?" I asked.

"O' course, it's what makes you a man. Once you get a fair amount in you, you'll start makin' some. Then you can have sons of your own. I did; your Pa probably did too. See how big n' strong he is? You wanna' be like him don't cha?"

It sounded like balderdash to me, but saw some twisted reasoning in this.

"All men have to get rid of it somehow," he continued to tell me. "Even if you don't fiddle with it, it'll come out at night when you're dreamin". Nightly emissions, they calls it. So, it's best to get it out ahead o' time. And it's more fun when you got a partner to help out. Like you done me," he added with a wink.

"Nightly emissions," I repeated to myself, slow like. I had to admit that I found his words sensible like, but I was still mystified. By then the afternoon had spilled into candlelight time, and it was time to get back.

~

GUY'S NEW TOYS

The eastern sky was an ocean of dark rambling clouds, brilliantly stained with crimson by the time Joe finally got onto the Eden's expressway heading home. Even at this hour, the traffic was heavy but the early morning air felt cold against his skin and helped keep him awake. His eyes, tired and red from lack of sleep, strained to focus, he thought about the past eight hours and how innocently the evening had started.

That afternoon he got a call from Guy, asking him to come over. Guy was a divorced father that he had gotten to know, and it had been a while since he'd heard from him. The man was always too busy with work or had his sons over, so Joe jumped at the chance to be able to see him again.

Joe met Guy one day while he was out walking his dog and cruising at a forest preserve on Golf Mill Road. He noticed Guy sitting on a bench getting some sun and thought he'd take a better look. He was just going to walk by when his dog decided at that moment to stop and squat down in front Guy and start to lick himself. Guy smiled and looked up, then nonchalantly said,

"Wish I could do that."

Joe seeing his chance, smiled devilishly and replied, "I think you'd better pet him first."

Guy gave Joe a puzzled look and laughed. "I meant on myself," he added.

"Oh, I know," said Joe, "but I've been dying to say that since I first heard that old joke."

"Yeah, real funny, you always use that as pick up line?"

"No, but it did work, don't you think?"

They laughed again and soon snuck off into the woods, and Joe sucked Guy for the first time. Later, they exchanged numbers and they saw each other whenever Guy had the time. Now Joe was anxious to see Guy again.

Joe drove to the gated community in the upscale neighborhood, pulled into the spot left for him, and walked up to the townhouse. He rang the door bell, expecting to see Guy, but instead was surprised when Mikey, Guy's eldest son answered the door.

"Joe, how are you doing, dude?" Mikey asked.
Joe met Mikey before and liked him, but wasn't prepared to see him just then.

"Hey, Bud!" Joe said putting out his hand to him. They shook hands and Mikey asked him in. "Where's the old man?" He asked then noticed Mikey was using his father's laptop. Right away Joe got alarmed and hoped Guy had encrypted or hid the files that they shared. A lot of them were pictures they had taken while having sex. Most were of Joe sucking Guy or getting fucked by him.

"He's in the bathroom," Mikey answered.

Then nervously Joe asked Mikey what he was doing.

"Not much. Just downloading some mp3's and stuff."

"Oh! Music files," Joe said. "Yeah, I love getting free stuff." They were discussing the files and what people thought about copyright laws and free domain, when Guy walked in.

"Hey Joey!" he said. "You made it."

But with Mikey's attention on the laptop, Joe mouthed; "How are we gonna fuck?" to Guy. Guy merely pointed to his son then brought his open cupped hand to his mouth, and smiled. Joe couldn't help his shit-eating grin, thinking about that actually happening. Then to Joe's surprise, and with Mikey's back to his father, Guy lowered the front of his sweat pants, exposing his cock just inches away from his son. Lewdly, he stuck his tongue out and fondled himself, and then, as if nothing out of the ordinary was happening, asked Joe if he wanted a drink.

"Yeah, sure," he answered dry mouthed. Mikey looked up to Joe with those innocent baby blues and smiled, oblivious to what his nasty father was up to. Of course Joe was shocked at how reckless Guy was being, but at the same, he was getting excited.

Joe knew that some men wanted to or had sex with their sons, and remembered being attracted to his own father, but they had never talked about this. He suspected that Mikey didn't know of his father's desire and now, Joe couldn't think of anything else. Guy and Joe went into the living room to talk; leaving Mikey to his mp3 downloads.

"Aren't you afraid he might open those pictures of us?" Joe asked.

"Naw, they're well hidden. Besides, even if he was to find them, do you really think he'd tell anyone? Or maybe you'd like that; him showing his buddy pictures of you sucking me?" He teased.

Joe had to admit; he liked the idea and started to get hard.

"Yeah, you know I would, you bastard, but what about the ones of you sucking me?"

"There aren't any," Guy said simply. "I deleted them. Besides I like looking at the ones of you," he said smiling devilishly.

"Bastard!" Joe hissed. Then Guy stood up and lowered his sweats again.

"Suck it!" he whispered. Guy didn't have to ask twice, but Joe was concerned about Mikey being in the next room and that he could walk in at any moment. Guy grabbed Joe's head, pulled him close then started talking about football and some upcoming game Joe knew nothing about. Guy was unusually loud so that Mikey could hear and not suspect what the men were actually doing. Of course, Joe wanted to forget about the boy being in the next room, to enjoy Guy's cock and to concentrate on sliding his lips up and down it sensuously. Suddenly, Joe heard Mikey move around in the kitchen and he froze. Then Mikey yelled to his father that he was going out.

"Ok," Guy yelled back. "Don't come back too late."

"Ok, Dad. See yah, Joe. Take care."

Then Mikey left, leaving Joe alone with Guy.

"Why didn't you tell me he was going to be home?" Joe asked Guy once they were alone.

"Sorry, but when I called you, I didn't know he was gonna be here. Besides he knows and likes you, what's the big deal? He's gone now and we can fuck."

"I guess," Joe said still feeling unsure. "But what if he comes back too soon?"

"Relax, he won't. He's probably going over to his buddy Jared's and when they get together and get into one of those online games, they're at it for hours. Anyway, I got some new toys we can play with," he said with a twinkle in his eye.

"Toys?" Joe repeated, surprised to hear this.

"Yeah, hold on a sec," Guy said. "I'll be right back." Then he disappeared into the other room and returned a short time later caring a fire-proof lock box. After unlocking it, he brought out something wrapped in what looked like faux red velvet. Inside were two items; a pair of flat-black handcuffs and a black leather mask, which looked like more of a blind fold, because there weren't any eyes openings.

"Ah huh!" Joe said, not knowing what to think. "And who's gonna be wearing these?" He asked, holding up the handcuffs. Guy merely looked at him, and without wanting to, Joe felt the corners of his mouth curl up into a silly grin.

Guy leaned towards Joe and kissed him gently while his fingers found Joe's nipples. Joe felt the gentle pinch and the familiar feeling of heat that spread throughout his body. He had to admit whenever anyone did that to him, all reason left him and he couldn't think straight. Guy found this out the first night, and was ready to take advantage of this simple fact.

Guy pulled Joe's shirt up, and in one smooth motion tore it off, then lowered his head to his chest and licked across

Joe's sensitive nipples. Guy nibbled, sending sharp waves of pleasure through the other man's body.

"Turn around," Guy ordered in a voice lower and softer than usual. Joe felt Guy's hot breath on the sensitive parts of his neck. He groaned in pleasure, feeling Guy's soft wet lips, the pressure, and the soft bite. He moaned again as his head fell back against Guy. The nearness of Guy, the coarseness of his chest hair, and his warmth lulled Joe into submission.

Joe felt Guy slip the mask over his head and cover his eyes. At first Joe jerked and resisted but Guy whispered into his ear, "Trust me."

His voice was soft and soothing. "Now, give me your hands," Guy whispered while nibbling at the other man's neck. Joe felt himself giving in, he couldn't resist.

Joe reached his hands behind and heard the jingle of the handcuffs before feeling the cold metal against his skin. He heard the click of the locking mechanism binding his hands together at the wrists. Why was he letting Guy do this?

"Too tight?" Guy asked. Joe hesitated then answered "no." Despite his reservations, Joe was enjoying the whole thing.

Guy nudged him forward, and Joe could tell that Guy had stood up. He heard the soft swoosh of cloth being pulled off Guy's body, then the unmistakable elastic sound of his jockstrap sliding down his hairy legs. Then Joe felt the soft cloth against his nose.

"Smell!" Guy ordered. Joe obeyed and inhaled deeply. The masculine scent of Guy's crotch was all over the jock.

"You like that?" Guy asked and Joe nodded yes. "Open your mouth." He was about to protest when he felt something being stuffed into his mouth. It was the musky jockstrap.

"Get up!" Guy commanded.

In pitch black darkness, Joe stood up and felt Guy fumble with his pants.

"Good," he said. "You wore your jockstrap like I told you. We'll leave your boots, I like that."

Joe felt Guy's warm mouth at his nipples again. He moaned despite the gag filling his mouth. Guy worked his way down to Joe's crotch and started sucking his cock. Joe didn't know how long Guy had been sucking other men's cocks, but he sure was good at it. He brought Joe to the brink of orgasm then stopped.

"Get up here," he said, but Joe couldn't tell what he meant so Guy nudged him forward again. "I want you to kneel down," he instructed, then guided Joe forward till his head was almost down against the coffee-tabletop. Joe felt Guy's tongue against his ass, wiggling its way in. He had gotten better at this, Joe thought. His tongue dug into Joe's hairy ass as his groans of delight filled the room.

Then Guy started teasing him with questions and fingering Joe's butthole as he spoke.

"Oh yeah, your ass is hot; hot and wet like a pussy. You like me eating your pussy, Joe?"

Joe could only nod his head. He licked it again and again, "Yeah, your pussy's hot," he said again. "hot and hungry."

Joe was uncomfortable with Guy referring to his ass as a pussy, but for now, Guy was right and he continued to tease Joe.

"Bet you'd like some hard cock to fill this hole, wouldn't you cock-sucker?" He asked, not expecting an answer. "Should I go next door and see if my neighbor Frank would want some of this?" He lewdly asked. "I'm sure both my neighbors on either side are home, and I'm sure they could use some willing cunt."

The thought of it along with Guy's insistent fingers was making it all seem so good.

"How about I go get you some cock, Joe, would you like that?" Guy asked then Joe heard him slip his sweats back on and leave.

At first he just lay there with head down against the table. *Where did he go?* Joe started to worry. Then an awful thought came to him; what if Mikey came home and found him this way? Joe attempted to push out the obstruction in his mouth, but heard something – whispering and what sounded like someone shushing. He wanted to ask if it was Guy, but all he could do is make muffled noises. He heard giggling; it had to be Guy. Was he pretending to have someone with him? Another wave of concern washed over him. What if it was the neighbor men? Suddenly Joe felt ashamed. Here he was blindfolded, butt-naked, and handcuffed. Worse of all, he was gagged with that damn, dirty jockstrap.

Joe heard muffled footsteps on the carpet coming nearer; someone was close. Suddenly a hand brushed against his back. It traced along his shoulder down his front and through his chest hair lightly. He felt someone lift him up and a warm mouth licking at his nipples. At the same time Joe felt another wet tongue at his ear. The sound of licking boomed in his ear. Then Joe heard another whisper; a soft indistinguishable voice.

"I'm going to remove the gag," it said close to his ear. "But I don't want you to say a word. You understand? Don't talk!"

It had to be Guy but at the same time Joe couldn't be sure. But reason told him it had to be Guy. Joe nodded his head yes, anything to be rid of the gag.

Joe felt the elastic strap rise over his head and the bundled pouch pulled from his mouth. Joe worked back the spit to his mouth made dry from the cloth, then started to say something but a hand covered his mouth.

"Remember, no talking!" the whisperer repeated. As the hand left Joe's mouth, the fingers lingered. Involuntarily, Joe licked at them. The fingers probed at his mouth, purposely, forcing their way inside. Then he felt a spongy softness against his lips and knew it had to be someone's cock. Instinctively, Joe opened his mouth; he came here wanting to suck cock, so he figured it must be one of Guy's neighbors. He only wished he knew what the man looked like. Although the cock in his mouth felt familiar, he wasn't sure if it was Guy's. Joe continued to slide his lips over the cock as he felt someone else's hand at the back of his head. That's when he heard the click of a camera; they were taking pictures. Joe started to protest but the cock down his throat stifled him. The only consolation was that his face was covered. But the suspense of who was here was getting to him. He had to find out who was here with Guy. He knew from the number of hands and cocks that there was indeed more than one man. Guy had to be one but who was the other?

The cock in his mouth continued to fuck his mouth. The room was filled with moans and soft whispers. The hands seemed to be all over, and the mouths bit and sucked at him. The sensations were delightful, but at some point Joe couldn't tell what was really happening. He lost sight or rather feel of who was where. Then someone's cock, larger this time, was at his butthole. His ass was slapped hard and the sound echoed through the room.

"Yeah, fuck him man," someone whispered. He wasn't gentle, that was for sure. With a grunt from Joe, it was shoved in almost to the hilt. He could feel it split and tear at his sphincter. He was being fucked at both ends now, incessant pounding at both holes. Then....

"Here give him some." Poppers were pushed under Joe's nose. They were fresh, powerful and he couldn't help but inhale deeply the industrial scent.

His body was all afire now with that warm feeling. The sound of pictures being taken echoed around him. His head swam and despite the cock lodged down his throat, he giggled and couldn't care less about who was here.

"Fuck me," he thought. *"Fuck my hairy pussy!"*

Then he realized he liked being like this. He was incapacitated and he loved it. He loved the feeling of total control. He was being fucked hard, and every so often someone slapped his ass again. More poppers were shoved under his nose, so powerful that they filled the room with the acidic scent. He was getting close. The cock popped from his mouth and he was able to sit back onto the hard cock wedged deep inside this ass.

"Oh, God, fuck me," Joe cried. "Yeah, yeah," he repeated.

"I'm gonna cum!" someone gasped.

"Who is that?" Joe wondered.

"Me too!" came another. Then Joe felt a hot wetness on his face and chest.

"Yeah?" he heard Guy say, flashes and the sound of the camera. "Cum in his pussy, fucker!"

Joe lapped at the hot shots of cum spitting out at him. Then he heard Guy next to him drenching him with cum also. The man behind Joe was cumming too. His cock slipped from Joe's ass, and the man stood up and finished on Joe's back.

After they had finished, Joe looked up. "I want to cum," he begged.

"Do you? How much do you?" Guy asked devilishly. Joe heard giggling around him.

"Come on, Guy," Joe begged "Enough's enough. Let me cum. Or at least, make me cum."

"Do you promise to be a good boy?"

"Yes, yes I promise."

"You know I was taking pictures again."

"Yeah, I know."

"You know what I'm gonna do with them?"

Joe shrugged his shoulders, seemingly defeated.

"I might show then to Mikey or let him 'accidentally' find them."

"Why would you do that? What kind of perverted thrill is it for you? He'd never talk to me again."

"Oh?" Guy quipped. Suddenly, he yanked the blind fold off.

At first the light blinded Joe but slowly, shapes began to form. Joe sat blinking, adjusting his eyes and looked up.

There towering over him were three figures; Guy, a young man he didn't know, and – oh my God – Mikey. They stood there looking down and smiling devilishly at him.

Then he realized it was Mikey who had just fucked him. Mike was the first to move; he bent down and helped Joe to his feet.

"You should have seen your face, Dude," he kidded. Joe didn't know what to say. He looked to Mikey then to Guy and finally to the new guy. He was younger then Mikey, dark and handsome.

"This is Jared," Mikey said. "Jared meet Joe."

Joe looked around still somewhat confused. Behind him Guy was unlocking the cuffs.

"Why the charade?" Joe asked.

"It was Dad's idea," Mikey said. "Yeah, we found all those pictures of you sucking dad. Dad and I have been messing round for a while now; since the divorce anyway. But actually, Dad caught me and Jared doing it, and after I found the pictures of you and dad, well, things just happened.

Joe rubbed his wrists, looking from one to the other. "That's all well and fine but I want to cum," he said wiping cum from his forehead. They all took hold of Joe and they laid him back down onto the sofa with Mikey between his legs.

"Suck his cock," Guy directed.

Jared was on Joe's side and began to suck and tease his nipple. Guy lay down next to Joe; "Surprise!" he said to him and smiled then began to kiss Joe as the boys serviced his buddy. Joe was in heaven and came quickly inside Mikey's mouth. Then the trio got down and cleaned Joe's stomach and face clean.

~

An Extra Pair
of Hands

It was early spring and Jake Rogers was outside planting shrubs. He had just taken his shirt off when he was interrupted by the familiar voice of his ex-sister-in-law, Carol. She was standing at the edge of the drive, waving her keys at him.

"Hi, Jake," she said with a bright smile. "I need to ask a big favor." She was dressed in business attire and looking very professional. "I need you to watch Reece for me," she added while pointing a thumb to the car behind her. Jake looked and saw Reece giving him a peace sign from the opened car window. He set down his tools and walked towards the over-smiling, bright-eyed woman. As he neared she tilted her head to one side and ever so lightly, ran a long brightly colored finger nail up and down his upper arm, teasingly.

"Please," she begged. "I have a last minute emergency and I don't have time to look for a sitter."

"A sitter?" he asked. "Don't you think he's old enough to take care of himself? He'll be graduating in a few months. Come on now; give the boy some credit."

"Yes, yes, I know. But not for two days," she admitted. "You know how boys his age are. Once I'm gone, he'll probably invite all his friends over and have a wild party. I don't want to come home to a frat-party aftermath. Besides, it looks like you could use an extra pair of hands around here. Please, please, please," she repeated.

Reece got out of the car, looking taller than he had the last time Jake had seen him. He was caring an overnight bag and dressed in an old, baggy school jersey and jeans.

"Hi Uncle Jake, dad was busy. Is it ok?" he said using his best charming smile.

"Damn," Jake thought. He was reluctant, but at the same time he was keenly aware of the feeling he had every time Reece was near.

"Yeah, sure, why not?" he finally said.

"Why don't you two have a good time and make it a bachelor's weekend?" Carol asked.

After some discussion; it was decided Reece would stay the weekend, provided he would indeed help out.

Before long Carol left and Jake got back to his planting. Having Reece there did come in handy, and the company detracted from the chores. As the afternoon moved on, the conversation centered on where the plants would go and how Reece was doing in school. Every so often Jake noticed the boy eyeing him, but pretended not to notice.

Sometime around six o'clock, they'd had enough. It had been a long strenuous day and even though he was used to lifting weights, Jake was sore. Getting older wasn't easy, even if you were keen on keeping fit.

After a quick shower, Jake felt refreshed and sexually charged. He put on a comfortable pair of loose fitting shorts, popped in a soft jazz CD, and started dinner, during which time, Reece showered. Jake tried to think of an excuse to go back into the bathroom, just to get a peek, but thought better of it. Then he looked down and noticed his crotch and how almost indecent it looked. And the more he thought; his cock lengthened and started to crawl down the leg of his shorts. He put on an apron to mask his excitement and concentrated on dinner. Soon Reece came in looking fresh and clean. His longish black hair was still somewhat wet and dangling down over his forehead, which made him look very sexy.

Once dinner was made, Jake took off the apron before sitting down. Reece noticed his uncle wasn't wearing underwear, and the boy's eyes widened involuntarily seeing the meaty crotch.

During dinner the boy acted coy and flirty, trying to impress Jake. He was overly animated and made hand gestures that were very suggestive. Jake was drinking beer, and Reece asked if he could have one, but promised solemnly, that he wouldn't tell. There was something in the way that Reece said he wouldn't tell, that brought a minute shiver up Jake's spine.

After taking a long sip of his uncle's beer, then another, Reece reached out and lightly brushed the hair on Jake's arm.

"Do you think I'll get this hairy," Reece asked innocently. Jake was taken aback and really didn't know what to say, but didn't pull away. He felt the warmth of the young man's touch and let it linger. Then the boy reached out further to his uncle's chest hair.

"Will I get this much hair on my chest too?" He teased. The boy just smiled innocently and continued to eat. Finally Jake said something.

"Well, your dad's hairy, so I imagine you will be, too, unless you take after your mother's side of the family."

"God, I hope not," Reece groaned. "All the men on my mom's side are bald."

After dinner, they retired to the living room to watch some TV. By now Jake was feeling even more tired and sore from the day's strenuous work and idly rubbed the back of his neck. Reece noticed and volunteered to give his uncle a massage.

"Oh man, would you?" Jake asked. "I'd love it if you really don't mind?"

"Sure not at all, least I can do for letting me stay the weekend." Jake took his shirt off and got down to the floor, face down. Reece in turn got on top of him, sitting on the small of his uncle's back; just over his butt.

His strong hands massaged his uncle's muscles methodically, doing one side then the other, being careful not to press or pinch too hard. Reece marveled at Jake's broad back. For an old guy, Uncle Jake was in great shape.

Jake felt the boy's warm hands lightly running over his bare skin. *"Nice,"* he thought. Jake was thinking of nothing other than how good it felt, and soon fell asleep. The next thing he knew, he woke suddenly and wondered where he was. He looked up and saw Reece sitting on the couch looking at him.

"You fell asleep," he said.

"How long have I been asleep?"

"Not long, maybe fifteen, twenty minutes."

"Guess I was more tired than I thought," he said, getting up and stretching.

"Ok, your turn."

Reece removed his shirt and shot down onto the floor without further urging. Jake did as Reece had done and sat on his nephew's butt. Jake's callused hands massaged Reece's soft skin, and he noticed how tight the young muscles were.

Jake inched his hands carefully and sensuously, teasing and tantalizing the young flesh. Sometimes, he'd glide his middle fingers, one after the other, down the boy's back bone, to just above his ass-crack, then back up and do it again.

This went on for about 15 minutes. Then with little effort, while the boy was relaxed, Jake slapped him hard on his ass, grabbed his legs, and in one swift movement, flipped the boy over onto his back. The boy grunted and looked up at his uncle with surprise and shame while trying to cover himself; he was hard, obviously from his uncle's expert touch. Jake merely shook his head and smiled demon-like. But Reece shrank, trying to hide his erection. Jake stood up, unbuttoned the top button of his jeans, and said he was going to bed. He left the room, leaving the boy to wonder what had just happened.

Jake was playing a game now; things were going better then he could have possibly planned. He changed into a crisp pair of white boxers and did two things before going to bed; he turned off the light and left the door open just a crack. Then he lay down on top of the comforter and waited.

It was quiet for some time; only the soft murmur of the TV in the living room as Jake fought to keep awake. He was thinking of what might happen, when he realized the TV had been turned off. He heard the unmistakable sound of a floor board creak just outside his door. Resisting the impulse to look, he lay very still and pretended to be asleep.

In the dim light he saw movement just outside the door. The shadow came and went, stopping several times. Then he heard the door being slowly pushed open.

Through half closed eyes, he saw his nephew cautiously inching his way towards his bed. Jake's heart pounded as the boy crossed the room and stood beside the bed. Soon, he felt the warm softness of the boy's hand barely gliding over his chest hair. A sinful thrill ran through him as the boy nervously explored. In a short time the boy got to Jake's crotch and felt for his uncle's hard cock. Jake tried but couldn't stand it any longer. While the boy was busy getting a good feel, Jake suddenly grabbed him by the wrist. Reece froze.

"You sure you want to do this?" Jake asked. "Is this what you really want?"

Reece was shaking now but didn't try to pull away. With every fiber of his being, he wanted to run away or curl up into a little ball and disappear. He didn't know what to say or how to answer. He felt his face burn and his heart stick in his throat. Then he stood up and gave in.

"Yes, I do," he answered finally. It was a small, meek answer, but an answer none the less. He admitted for the first time that this was indeed what he wanted to do. For as long as he could remember, his uncle had been the source of his sexual fantasies. Jake was the kind of man he wanted to become. He loved his father, but his uncle was all man. He was big and tough, brutally handsome and self-reliant. He looked up to Jake and admired him more than anyone else. Now, here he was, a child again, caught with his hand in the proverbial cookie jar.

"Ok," Jake simply said. "Lie down next to me."

Reece complied, but first removed his jeans. Even in the semi-darkness Jake could see that he was only hairy from the waist down: probably the reason for him not wanting to take his jeans off earlier.

It was awkward at first, but before long, they embraced and locked in a deep kiss.

"It's funny," Jake thought, *"here I am French kissing my nephew."*

It was wrong, he knew, but felt so good. Sin or not, the body in his arms felt so right. He mustn't think of Reece as a relative or his little brother's only son. He was just another man; a very hot young man.

Jake was on Reece's side as the boy lay under him. Jake slid his calloused hand over Reece's firm chest, and Reece shivered as if cold.

"Relax son. I won't hurt you, and we won't do anything you don't want to do," Jake continued.

"Oh, Uncle Jake, we can do anything. I've wanted this for so long I don't know where to start."

"I know Reece, I know," Jake confided, then reached over and turned on the side light. "There that's better, now we can see what we're doing," he said to Reece, but really more to himself.

Jake gazed down to the boy beneath him and thought *"My god he was magnificent."* He'd looked at his nephew many times, but not like this. Now he was able to really look closely and without having to be careful that someone might notice.

"Lift your arms," he instructed.

Reece obeyed and lifted both arms over his head, and Jake locked them together in a one handed grasp. With the other he ran it teasingly over Reece's smooth chest and lightly pinched the boys left nipple.

"Oooooo," Reece cooed. The boy squirmed with pleasure from the expert handling he was getting. Jake continued down the boy's flat belly *"Oh, to have abs like this,"* Jake thought. Then followed the wispy hair line to the boy's cock; steel-piston hard and ready for attention. Without hesitation, he brought this face close to the boy's crotch. Reece lifted his head in time to see his uncle lick then engulf his cock.

"Oh God," he groaned, setting his head back. He felt the warm wetness of his uncle's mouth and couldn't believe he was here now after so many years of wanting this. He'd had male sex before, but not with anyone that was older than his father, and certainly not with anyone more expert at making love than this.

Jake slid his wet lips across the sensitive skin of the boy's cock, and then took it deep into his throat. For added effect, he let it stay for a moment while massaging the spongy head against back of this throat.

Once Jake released Reece's arms, the boy was able to scoot down and take his uncle's cock and bring it to his lips.

"Ok, Reece, you've wanted to get at it all night; here's your chance."

The boy smiled sheepishly as wasted no time in getting between his uncle's long hairy legs. At first he was a little unsure of the extra skin, but before long, he was enjoying the feel. Jake held the boy's head close, entwining his thick fingers through Reece's long hair. He looked down, and images of Reece at different ages of his life came to him. Flashes of birthdays, baseball uniforms, summer swims, and camping trips came to mind, now here they were grown and more intimate than they ever could have been. Jake loved the boy like his own, but unlike the boy's dad, Jake had secretly wanted this. Now that the boy was old enough and able to make his own decisions, it was the perfect time.

Reece continued to suck, using both hands along with his lips, trying hard to make it feel right for his uncle. He found it easy to do with the added foreskin.

"Yeah, that's it Reece," Jake uttered. He was enjoying all that Reece was doing but he wanted to taste more of the boy, so he pulled Reece up to his face and kissed him again. Now they were on their knees, face to face. Jake overtook Reece and got him back down onto the bed. He kissed again, down the boy's front, and continued over his balls then maneuvered himself between the boy's hairy legs. With each of the boy's ankles in his fists, he brought them up and over Reece's head. Jake looked down greedily at the boy's exposed ass, then sank his face down onto Reece's virgin butthole and proceeded to devour it. At first he just lapped, but soon he was tunneling his tongue further and further into the boy's pucker hole. Reece was moaning and thrashing his head about.

"Oh, fuck," he kept moaning. Jake kept digging and sucking at the warm hole. He'd let up, spit smeared and see the boy's ass lips quivering from the attention; it was clenching and unclenching like a carp out of water. His ass was silky smooth and Jake couldn't help but slam his tongue back into it again and again. Reece moaned and melted from the tongue fucking he was getting. Then Jake got into position. The boy looked up, wide eyed and anxious.

"Yes," he cooed.

"You want it?" Jake asked. "Tell me."

"Yes," Reece answered again.

"Come on, tell me!" Jake commanded. "I want to hear you beg for it. What do you want?"

"Fuck me, Uncle Jake. I want you to fuck me, please," he begged.

"Good boy, that's what I wanted to hear."

Then Jake took his cock and brought the head to the boy's waiting ass. He pushed and slowly sank into the velvety softness of the boy's innards. Reece's eyes grew wider as the hooded cock slid into him. He groaned between clenched teeth, then held his breath and sighed deep and long. Before he realized, it was in balls deep, and he could feel his uncle's wiry pubes against his soft ass cheeks.

"Good boy," Jake said, "Suck it up into your hole."

Reece didn't know if what was he was doing was right or not, but it felt good. Then Jake started the carnal movements of lust; in and out slowly and purposely. His hard cock slid across the sensitive skin of the boy's pucker hole, causing not pain but unbelievable intense sensations. Reece wiggled his toes in response. His ass was being forced open. He tried to push out, but he couldn't.

"It's like taking a shit," he was once told.

"God," Reece thought. *"Like taking a big-ass shit."* The sensations were really getting more intense now. He found himself whimpering; almost crying. The whole room echoed with his cries.

"Oh, Lord, Uncle Jake, fuck me," Reece whimpered. "Oh, oh, oh," he cried with each powerful thrust.

"Take it Reece. Take it son," Jake begged.

Then, at long last, there was a high pitched squeal, along with a drawn out cry as they came together. Each groaned and cried, and then Jake fell on top of the boy. They kissed gently, still with the older man's cock buried deep inside. After a time Jake said,

"I'm gonna take it out, but don't worry, I'll take it slow."

Reece clenched his teeth and squinted his eyes as if someone were pulling a log from his body. There was a loud obscene pop as it freed itself.

"Oohhh, damn," he sighed.

"You ok?" Jake asked.

"Yeah, I think so."

Then they both laughed and kept laughing. It was funny, but for the life of the man and his nephew, they didn't know exactly why.

~

BLESS ME FATHER

"Bless me Father, for I have sinned," I said, reciting the age old prayer for absolution. Kneeling in the tiny dark confessional of St. Michael's, I worried what my father confessor would think. "It has been two weeks since my last confession," I continued.

I itemized a list of mortal and venial sins to the old priest, starting with the most severe: missing mass on Sunday, eating meat on Friday, and then came the juicy part.

"And I played with myself six times," I lied. Actually, it had been more like ten or sixteen, but who actually keeps count. It's not like you write it down on a calendar or anything; cut a notch on your bed post, or you're on some plan and have to keep track.

Also this has always puzzled me; does God really care if you master bate? If so, why? Anyway, I figured I'd just double the penance and it would be all right. If he told me to say five "Our Fathers" and five "Hail Mary's," I'd just say more. I was pretty sure God would understand.

"And I had bad thoughts, Father," I shyly added.

"What kind of thoughts, my son?" he asked.

"Well, Father, it was more like nasty thoughts."

"Oh?" he asked. "What kind?"

"It's hard for me to say, Father; I'm embarrassed," I said to him, not really sure of how to put it.

"It's ok my son. It's only through my ears to God's."

"Ok, Father. I have nasty thoughts about one of my neighbors."

"Who is this girl?" He asked.

"Um... It's not a girl, Father."

"Oh? Is it a boy?" he asked again, seemingly more interested.

I hesitated at first. "It's a man, Father, Mr. Riley."

Silence....

"I see. What do you think about?" he asked.

"I think about his... thing, Father."

"His thing, you mean his penis?"

"Yes, Father," I answered shyly. From his side of the cubical, I heard him move.

"What do you think about?"

"Well, actually, Father, I think about touching it again."

"Again?" he asked with a gasp. "Have you touched it before?"

"Yes, Father. Twice before," I said waiting for his response.

"You know, my son. You have to tell me everything! You can't leave anything out or you may not be absolved."

"OK, Father," I answered. "One day I saw him playing with his thing."

"You mean his cock?"

"Yes, Father his...cock."

"How was it that you were able to see that?" he asked.

"I heard my father talking to my mom about him. She had mentioned him, and he said he was a cock sucker. Oh, sorry, Father. I mean that he was queer, and I got curious and started thinking more and more about him. I'd see him out on his lawn or at the store. I didn't think he looked queer, he looked normal. Then one night I went over to his house and peeked in his windows and saw him."

"Saw him doing what?" Father asked.

"I saw him playing with himself... um... jacking off. He was watching movies with just men in them, and when I thought he got up to go to the bathroom; he came out and caught me. I guess I was jacking off too."

"What do you mean, you guess. Didn't you realize what you were doing?" he asked.

"Well, Father, I got excited seeing him that way."

"And what got you excited about him?"

"I guess it was the size of his cock, Father, it was big."

"I see. How big would you say it was? Seven inches, eight inches, what?"

"I'm not sure, but it was huge and thick. When he was sitting it came up to his chest."

"Oh my, that is big. And that's what made you want to touch it?"

"I guess so, Father. After he caught me and saw I was playing with myself, too, he looked around and asked if I wanted to come inside and watch the movies with him."

As I was telling Father my tale, I heard him shifting and moving within his side of the cubical. Through the partition, I could see his silhouette. He seemed to be fidgeting.

"Then what happened?" By the sound of his voice I could tell he was getting nervous.

"Well, Father, we sat on the sofa and he showed me more of his nasty movies, and then he asked if I wanted to touch him."

"Did you?" he asked anxiously.

"Yes, Father, I did," I answered.

"So, did he force you to anything else?"

"Oh no Father, he didn't make me do anything. I wanted to really."

"And what else did he do? Did he touch you?"

"Yes Father, he did and he kissed me. As I was holding his cock our faces were close and he kissed me on the lips. It wasn't bad, Father. He didn't make me, but he stuck his tongue into my mouth too. Oh, God, Father, I... I liked it. Then he took my clothes off and... and..."

"What son? What did he do to you?" By now he sounded almost out of breath.

"He told me to lie back, and he got on top of me and put his head close to me and took my dick into his mouth. And, Father, it felt really good," I added.

Slowly, the little door separating us slid open. The old priest was standing up. His cassock was open with the zipper to his dark trousers open.

"My son you're going to have to show me. I still don't have a clear idea of what you mean," he said sounding nervous. "Go ahead reach in."

I felt funny doing this, even though I was excited. I never thought about him in this way. Timidly, I reach over and felt his crotch.

"Oh, my!" I gasped.

"What the matter, son?" he whispered.

"Nothing, Father, it's just that you're so big; a lot bigger than Mr. Riley's."

"I see," he said. "Now demonstrate to me what you did." In the dim light of the confessional, his cock looked huge. It had a perfectly formed head that was rather wide, and hung at an angle from its own weight. The extra skin covered over about half the crown. I marveled at it, thinking it was different from Mr. Riley's and fatter too. I ran my fingers along the veins, tracing the lines. It jumped and pulsed at my touch. I noticed a drop of pre-cum had formed at the piss hole.

"Go ahead, son. Don't be afraid. Show me!" He whispered. I licked at the head; it jumped again, hitting my nose. Then I wrapped my hand around its wide circumference, holding it in place and brought it to my mouth. His cock was warm and the skin soft like silk. It had a clean sort of incent smell to it and the head filled my mouth entirely.

"Ooh!" I heard him gasp. As I stretched my lips around it, he pushed it forward, shoving more of it in.

"Uumph!" I grunted.

"Do exactly as you do with your neighbor" he hissed. I did as I held his cock at the base, like a club. Then I wondered that if this wasn't a sin, too. But I was enjoying it too much as I felt myself responding and getting hard. I wondered also that if I took out my cock and jacked off, would this be a sin as well?. But I reasoned that since I was in the confessional and with the priest, it would be alright. All I was doing really was confessing my sins, but demonstrating them might be the clincher.

I slid my wet lips along the long thick shaft as my mouth stretched to accommodate its size. The sounds of my slobbering demonstration filled the cramped space, as I felt the spit run down my chin.

"Oh, Lord!" I heard Father praying, "That's it!"

He was asking God to forgive my sins, as he ardently shoved his cock into my face.

"Humph!" his shoving was getting urgent, and he was breathing hard.

I liked the feeling of it in my mouth and applied pressure to the head, trying to suck up some of the spit. Then without realizing it, I was lost in the rhythm of it all. I sank further to my knees, and felt like a baby sucking a bottle. It was euphoric. I felt so content, so calm. The feel of his huge cock in my mouth was comforting. Yes, like a pacifier. I found myself absorbed in it, taking in as much of it as I could. The old priest was praying for me, bless him, but I couldn't hear him. All I could think about was his cock and what it meant to me. I sucked in; breathing through my nose. My head moved up and down over the smooth hard pole. The kneeler I was on rocked to and fro as it bounced on the polished marble floor. I held on to the sides of the opening, trying to steady myself, while he rhythmically fucked my face. I could feel his cock pulse, getting ready to shoot. I braced myself, I knew what was coming. I found myself wanting it. I sucked harder and faster.

"That's it son!" He was saying in a hoarse whisper. "Show me. Show me! Oh, God! Show me!"

I had to hold on, trying to keep up. I felt the first explosion and recognized the taste. My mouth filled with the spunky liquid, more and more then I had to swallow. The taste was slightly different then Mr. Riley's, maybe it was holy or something. I didn't know. After his wild thrusts he withdrew, pulling his cock from my eager mouth. Reluctantly, I let go and had to suck up the stray spit it had produced. Already it was getting soft, but glistened with the combination of my spit and his cum.

He quietly and slowly slid back the little door, sat down, sighed then told me to be a good boy and to say a few Hail Mary's. He sounded relaxed then added that next time I would tell him my sins in the rectory, behind that alter.

Then to my amazement, he asked if I ever wanted to be an altar boy. But, I was still very excited, and I wanted to jack off badly. I left St. Michael's and went straight to Mr.

Riley's, hoping he'd be home. I wanted to rack up a few new sins to demonstrate to my father confessor.

~

THE GHOST OF DARK OAK COTTAGE

Journal, 30th October

The morning has come, but has not helped in making it clearer, so I write for fear I am losing my mind. I will say, that the events that transpired are, by no means, idle dreams or wishful thinking on the part of one who has gone without for so long. Maybe in the writing, I will be able to make some sense of it all. I only hope that whoever finds this will not judge me too harshly and understand why I did what I did and what brought all this on. I will start at the beginning, and try as I might to put down all that I have experienced. I pray that the Almighty will forgive me and take pity on a weak soul.

Just having ended an exhaustive month, my dealings with clients were, shall we say, less than fruitful. In my need for solitude and rest, I scoured the advertisements in hopes of finding the perfect hide away. I had almost given up all hope and was about to shuck the whole idea when I happened upon a small obscure advertisement.

"Rest in Peace," it read which I found a bit odd, "Sleepy, turn-of-the-century cottage on large estate waiting for the right person."

I wrote immediately for more information as there was no number to call and in less than a week a small parcel arrived, inside was a handwritten letter along with a few old yellowed photographs. The letter was as follows:

Dear Sir,

I am pleased at your request to see my cottage. It has been in my family for generations and in need again for life. Dwellings must have occupants to live, and without them they wither and die. I cannot myself live within these premises for reasons I cannot go into here. I trust you will require it as soon as possible. Please see enclosed photos as I am sure you will find what you are looking for. I look forward to further correspondence with you.

Sincerely,

D. O'Donnell, Esq.

I examined the photographs with relish, and one struck me with the vague thought of a memory long forgotten. The image was a picturesque tiny lodge concealed in ivy. The porch was draped over with hanging ferns, spider plants, and what looked like flowering impatiens, so much so, that almost everything was obscured. I couldn't help feeling there was something familiar, yet sad about the place. The other photo was the interior of the cozy looking living area with overstuffed couches and a large hearth that dwarfed the small space. I came to a quick decision to secure the old place, and wired the proprietor that I would accept his offer.

By the next week's end I began my journey early at day break, motoring along a scenic route in hopes of taking in the fall color. The day was dazzling in its production of vivid color; akin to a forest fire consuming the valleys and ridges. I drove at a moderate pace; enjoying the day and watching as the brilliant scenery zoomed passed me in blurs of color. Soon I felt my frayed nerves start to calm.

Autumn has always been my favorite time of the year. There is a rather odd sense, to me anyway, about the aroma of burning leaves in the cool crisp air and the shortening daylight hours, that sets my soul to revel in the bliss of twilight thought. I must confess that I have always been, and probably shall always remain, a hopeless romantic.

The instructions given me were undemanding, as for once, I hadn't lost my way. I turned off the main road, per instructions, at a stone and iron gate. About a mile in, I came to a smaller side road where I was to turn right. It was now approaching dark, and I was alarmed as the road seemed to close in on either side, but just as I was about to turn back, I came to a picturesque covered bridge. Beyond that, about a mile in, was the old cottage. I was neither surprised nor troubled that it looked little different from the old photographs shown to me. As I neared, I noticed a large man, who I assumed was Mr. O'Donnell, sitting on one of the two Adirondack chairs that flanked the entrance way and waved to me as I approached. I parked on the gravel drive way as the sun was about to set.

As I approached, I noticed his piercing gray eyes, and I couldn't help feeling that we had met before. *"Wonderful,"* I thought, *"this could prove to be very interesting."* His big hands engulfed mine as we shook hands and I could tell he was sizing me up as well.

"Ah, Sir, I was starting to get worried. You know those roads can be a bit tricky, if you aren't used to them." As he spoke he tilted his cap back a bit, exposing his closed cropped silver hair.

He told me that, "the Mrs.," as he called her, had made supper, and it was warming in the oven.

"There won't be any way of getting hold of me, so I'll drop by every so often. We live just up the road." I knew that the house didn't have phone service. That was one reason for taking it.

"There won't be anything tonight." I assured him. "I just want to have dinner and early to bed."

"I can understand that!" he remarked and got into his old truck and disappeared down the road. I stood there and looked around. An uneasy feeling came over me and a shutter slithered up my spine. I suddenly felt very alone.

"I wish he would have stayed a little longer." I said to myself. I felt silly. *"Get a hold of yourself, old man. This is the country and it's going to get a lot darker."*

I went into the cottage, and immediately a wonderful smell of freshly baked bread and dinner in the oven overtook my senses.

My nose guided me past the dining room, which was fully laid out for dinner, and into the small cozy kitchen. My dinner was in the oven, waiting for me just as Mr. O'Donnell said. I hurried to put my bags away and soon found myself at the table. I opened a bottle of wine and ate my wonderful homemade meal with so much enthusiasm that I soon forgot about my lonely feeling. After dinner, I built a fire in the oak mantled fireplace and settled into an overstuffed chair. A wind had picked up, and with it, the threat of a storm. I smiled to myself and sank further down into the chair as it seemed too perfect for this Gothic setting.

I sat reading *Interview with the Vampire* by Anne Rice and continued to drink my wine. I was at the chapter where Claudia, the child vampire, has just presented Lestat, the older of the two other vampires, with two young boys, drunk on poison-laced wine.

Nestled in the comfortable chair and sleepy with wine myself; I started to doze. The tranquil, quiet of the old place surrounded me. Only the sounds of the crackling fire, the old mantle clock and the moaning wind outside existed to me. I was having difficulty reading through heavy eye lids and thought I could smell a faint sweet scent; like chrysanthemum flowers. The scent was unmistakable. In my half sleep, I was dreaming; I could see and feel the presence of the child vampire. I smiled to myself, thinking how sometimes my dreams were so vivid, when I realized it wasn't a little girl but a boy. He stood there in the corner shadows, white faced and watching me. His brilliant blue eyes reflected the light and seemed to burn with incandescent fire.

He was dressed in a plain white night shirt, holding a candle, as though ready for bed. His halo of golden curls framed his angelic face. He made one step forward and smiled. He was about to speak, when suddenly, "BARROOM;" clap of thunder jolted me awake and the boy was gone.

At first I was a little tangled in my thoughts and wondered where I was. I thought it funny, but the faint aroma of chrysanthemums still lingered.

"Am I still dreaming?" I thought to myself. I got up to stretch and pressed my hands to my crotch and realized I had an erection. I pressed again, oh that wonderful feeling. The boy came to mind and I smiled to myself, *"Strange dream."*

I retired upstairs, built another fire in the master bedroom fireplace, and continued to drink my wine before going to bed. It was deliciously warm, and I decided to sleep nude. The autumn storm bellowed outside as the wind and rain tested the window panes, but I felt safe and secure. The half bottle of wine had made me wonderfully horny. I felt aroused as I stretched out on the canopy bed.

"Now, if only I had a man to sleep with." I told myself. *"Handsome Mr. O'Donnell would do nicely."* I thought.

I rubbed my hairy chest and teased my nipples, thinking about Mr. O'Donnell. My hand went down further to my cock and squeezed it between my fingers. I half started to masturbate, wondering what it would be like to be in his arms, but soon drifted off into a soothing sleep.

The old Swiss clock downstairs chimed midnight. I slowly opened my eyes, not quite fully awake. I lay there in a half sleep with my eyelids heavy. Through the window, a silvery shaft of pale moonlight floated across the floor and onto the bed. The dying fire crackled softly. A soft draft came up and disturbed the gathered dust there on the floor. The particles of dust danced in the moonlight as they slowly swirled and began to collect, becoming dense. I watched in fascination as it seemed to be taking on some sort of form. At first it was indistinguishable, then before my eyes, the boy in the nightshirt appeared. This had to be a dream. The boy seemed to have materialized from thin air.

Again, he was holding a candle. Slowly, cautiously, he approached and stood by the bedside. I was still on my back and uncovered.

"Oh Lord!" I thought to myself; I was still naked. The boy seemed not to have noticed. I knew it was inappropriate, I was embarrassed and tried to cover myself, but found I could not move. Leaning over me, the boy looked closely into my face. His brilliant blue eyes seemed to glow with an inner light, and again, the scent of chrysanthemums, clean and fresh.

"Papa?" he whispered. His voice was so sweet and it sent such a thrill to me that I thought I'd faint. He looked down to my nakedness and giggled; a clear silvery bell of a laugh.

"I've been searching for you," he said with such innocence.

He set the candle down onto the night table and wrapped his arms around his upper body.

"Papa, I'm so cold. May I get in with you?" he pleaded.

"Yes." I said but still asleep.

With a soft cottony whoosh, he slipped his nightshirt off and crawled in beside me. He wrapped his soft arms around me and enveloped me like a warm, summer breeze. It was such a wondrous feeling and I couldn't believe I was dreaming this. Lightly he brushed the hair on my forehead.

"Where have you been, Papa? You said you'd be back in a short time and I've been so lonely all this time." he told me.

At first I didn't know what to say, but found I still couldn't move.

"It's ok, you're fine now," I reassured him. Then he bent down and softly kissed each of my eye lids. Somehow, I knew the boy's name: Joshua.

I was very excited, but also ashamed that I was giving into his exploration. He examined my chest as his hands ran though the hair and at the same time he kissed my neck.

165

The feeling was exquisite and it sent a thrill throughout my body that I will never forget. Then, with the clap of thunder and lightning, I came; a climax that shook the whole bed. I woke up with a jolt. I was alone and realized I'd had shot all over myself. I looked around to see where he'd gone, but he had vanished; it was only a dream.

The fire had died and with it so had the storm. *"Joshua."* I said to myself.

31st October, Saturday

In the morning, the sun was shining brightly after last night's storm. But with the sun came reality. I got up and showered, but no amount of washing could remove last night's happening. I was sure it was a dream. I busied myself with reading, drawing and some wandering and soon forgot the whole thing ever happened.

Sometime later, Mr. O'Donnell came by. I was sitting on the front porch reading, when I heard his old pickup drive up. I looked up to see him get out and come over to me. He was wearing snug fitting chinos and a polo shirt with a flannel shirt over that. Coming closer, I saw that he hadn't shaved that morning. He looked rugged and handsome. He also wore a different cap that was more of a baseball type.

"Morning sir," he said enthusiastically.

"Good morning!" I repeated. "Please call me Nick," I insisted.

"All right, Nick, only if you call me David."

"Deal!" I agreed.

"How did you sleep?" he asked. "Did the storm keep you awake?"

"Oh, no, not at all, I slept like the proverbial baby, but it did give me strange dreams," I said, recalling the dream-boy. I offered him a cup of coffee. He accepted and we went into the cottage. Sitting at the kitchen table, we talked about the weather, a bit of politics, mostly polite chatter. As he spoke, I realized I wasn't even listing to anything he was saying. I couldn't help noticing those deep gray eyes, those big hands, and his way of looking directly at me as he spoke. All at once, I realized he was repeating, "Nick, Nick, you ok?"

"Huh? Oh, I'm sorry. I, ah, was just, ah, daydreaming I guess." He seemed a little hurt.

"That's all right; my wife says I have a way of rattling on. She just ignores me at times."

"Oh, no, it's not the company. You are, by no means, a boring man. Not with those eyes. It's just that I have something on my mind." He blushed as he looked down to his coffee. Self consciously, he brushed back the side of his hair with his right hand.

"I'm sorry. I've embarrassed you," I said. "I do have a way of saying what's on my mind. Pay me no mind."

"Wish I could be like that," he said, feeling more at ease. "At times there are things I'd like to say or do." We fell into silence for a while. Together, we both started to speak then stopped in unison. We laughed.

"Your face sure does light up when you smile," he suddenly said. Now, I was feeling self conscious.

"I... I dish out complements with no trouble; I just don't know how to take them."

"Well then, I guess we're equal," he said to me, smiling. "You mentioned a dream earlier," he asked. "This place holds many memories; some happy, some sad. Mostly happy ones, I assure you."

"It wasn't a nightmare," I said, remembering the dream. "It was a pleasant, I think." I felt my cock stir. "There was," I paused a moment, not knowing how to put it "Someone in my dream; a boy."

"Oh?" he said looking up at me. "A boy?" His eyes were wide with interest. "You saw the boy?"

"*The* boy?" I repeated. "You mean you know about him? How could you know about the boy who I dreamt about only last night?"

"I don't want to frighten you, and I should have mentioned it before, but that wasn't any dream," he said, as he leaned in closer to my face.

"What? What are you trying to say? That a kid got into here last night, and got into..." He smiled again.

"You're not going to believe this but it was a..."

"A ghost?" I interrupted.

"Yes, you saw a ghost!" he assured me. "You saw a ghost of a boy long since dead."

I sat in silence for a while, trying to take it all in.

"You're shitting me, right?" I asked him. "Pardon my French but I mean, it was just a dream. A very pleasant one I might add, but just a dream."

"No." he said, "I've seen him too. I've slept in the same bed." Suddenly we were both embarrassed, thinking about the other.

"He usually doesn't take to strangers, and certainly doesn't make himself known to them. Did he, ah, get in bed with you?" he asked shyly.

"Yes!" I said rather shyly. For a long time we looked at each other. My heart started to pound loudly in my chest, and my mouth was getting dry. Suddenly we heard a crash from the other room. I looked at him in surprise.

"What the..."

He looked at me.

"I think we have company," he said smiling.

We both looked in the direction of where the noise had come from; together we got up and moved to the front room. Nothing seemed out of place to me, but I wasn't familiar with where things should or shouldn't be.

We sat down again, this time in the living room. David was sitting by the fireplace. He picked up an old tintype picture in an ornate silver frame and handed it to me.

"Here, look!" he said. "Look familiar?" I stood and took it from him.

"Oh my God!" I gasped. "It's him." I couldn't believe what I was seeing. It was a picture, decades old of the boy wearing a sailor suit and standing out in front of the cottage. Suddenly, I felt as though something had pushed me and lost my balance; I toppled into David's lap.

"I'm sorry," I apologized. "I don't know what happened." I was in his arms, my face so close to his. I could feel his breath on me.

We fell again into silence. His face moved closer to mine as he brought his hand behind my head and brought it up to his. Our lips touched, we kissed, I felt his tongue push into my mouth, and I gladly accepted. From somewhere, there came an impish giggle.

"What was that? Did you hear that?" I asked.

David looked around, listening, but seemed not really surprised, nor was he alarmed.

"I've got to get back," he said suddenly.

"Wait a minute," I protested. "You can't just come in and tell me there's a ghost in here, not to mention sticking your tongue down my throat, and leave as though nothing's happened."

"Would you like me to come back later, this evening?"

"What about the boy?" I asked "Who is he? What does he want?"

"I can't go into all that now," he said as he was getting up. "I promise to tell you everything tonight."

I agreed and led him out the front door and watched him drive away again.

Throughout the day, I kept thinking of David. I couldn't believe my luck. Here I was, practically in the middle of nowhere. And just down the road, was a man who was just the type of man that I enjoyed. And he was interested in me, to boot.

The boy was another matter. I didn't know quite what to make of it.

"A ghost?" I asked myself. David knew of him. If it were a dream, could we have both dreamt of the same person, on the same bed?

"Not likely!" I said out loud.

Alone again, I felt a bit uneasy knowing someone might be watching, especially a boy. I wasn't afraid, I was just very aware of his presence. Nothing else extraordinary happened after that first incident. I wasn't sure of all this. I had paranormal experiences before, but nothing like this.

With all that happened that afternoon, I decided to have a light dinner, consisting of bread, cheese, a glass of wine, and cold chicken. It seemed appropriate.

The mantle clock struck 6 o'clock as the sun was about to set. I sat on the porch and watched as it sank low on the horizon. A feeling of melancholy came over me as the colors of the day turned to a deep red, then purple - Twilight. My heart seemed to sink with the sun. Wistfully, I gazed up the road. I longed to see that old pick up come rambling up.

31st, October, Later

I write this as he lies beside me. I woke up full of energy. I can't believe what happened. I don't want to get ahead of myself.

Eventually, David did come back. I stood before him, awkward at first, not knowing just how intimate I could be with him.

"Come here!" he said, sensing my hesitation. He reached out for me and took me into his arms. "I've been thinking of you ever since I left here, Nick. Do you realize how hard it is to find a man like you? Especially around here, I've been married for a long time and I love my wife. There is just another side to me. A side you seemed to have picked up on. I wouldn't have ever, not in a million years, acted on it."

He kissed me long and hard. How such a man could go unnoticed around here was beyond my comprehension.

Then without much effort on his part, He lifted me. I'm not a heavy man, but David is not a young one. He must be well into his sixties. He carried me upstairs to the master bedroom and set me down on the bed. He stood back and just looked at me. I was feeling a bit strange, so I started to undress.

"No! Let me do that," he pleaded. I was seated on the edge of the bed, legs over the side. He knelt between them. I was wearing an old, red flannel shirt. He unbuttoned it, working his way down. He pulled off my white cotton tee, and then ran his hand across my chest, seemingly enjoying the feel of the hair. He fumbled with my belt buckle and undid my jeans.

"Lift up!" he instructed. I leaned back on my elbows and watched as he pulled them off. He gazed at me smiling. I was left in my boxers, legs spread wide. "You have the hairiest legs I've seen in a long time," he said running his hands over them.

"Yeah, my daddy gave them to me as a puberty present," I joked.

"How old is your father?" he asked.

"Oh. I'd say he was your age," I lied as I watched him take off his shirt and buttoned undershirt. He had broad shoulders and a chest hairier that mine. I noticed self consciously that I had more of a belly then he did. In other words, he looked great. I sat up and put my arms out and he came to me, I placed the right side of my face on his stomach. He wrapped his arms around me and held me close.

He pulled me to standing position and turned me around, facing away from him. He pulled my boxers off. Again he wrapped his arms around me and kissed my neck. I leaned my head to one side so he could easily get at it, at the same time pinching my nipples. We got into bed side by side.

"I'm going to tell you something about the boy." I started to speak but he interrupted. "I know, I know." He said. "Just let me finish. You find this all hard to believe but believe me, the boy is real. He died years ago. I think in my grandfather's time. His name is…"

"Joshua," I said before he could tell me. His eyes widened again.

"So, he does come to you?" he asked. "I saw him for the first time years ago when I inherited the place. I was here repairing a few things, and one night it got late, so I stayed here. I slept in this bed. He came to me that first night. I thought, like you, that it was a dream. I had never done anything like that with a man, although I had thought about it. Maybe all men do, but that night he was all over me, not physically. I can't explain it. I saw him standing in the moon light."

"Me too!" I added.

"He had the most incredible presence. I lay here and he came to me. Before I knew it, I had a powerful sensation between my legs. My cock pumped up to the biggest I'd ever seen. I swear I could see his head between my legs. Then it was as though he was sitting on it. As he moved up and down on it, I could feel my nipples being pinched. And no one ever did that, before or since."

"What do you know of him?" I asked, idly stroking David's cock.

"I believe he's searching for his father. I don't know if he abandoned him or the father was killed while away. I think he's searching for the love of his father. I'm not sure how the boy died."

David fell silent and looked away, thinking. Again I was filled with pity for the boy.

"So alone," I said half to myself. David pulled me close and we kissed. We were involved, when all at once; I noticed the fresh scent of chrysanthemums. David noticed it, too.

"Are you with us?" he asked out into the dim light. A slight breeze blew in from nowhere.

"He's here!" David announced.

I turned to look behind me. There beside the bed stood the boy, just a vague image, barely visible.

"Hi, Josh!" David said looking past me.

"Hello, Daddy," said the sweet voice. So clear it could almost break your heart. Now I knew this wasn't a dream for sure.

"How's my boy?" David asked him. Like a gaseous form, the boy passed me and over to David. He tilted his head back slightly and closed his eyes.

"Mmmmm," he cooed. I watched as David slowly leaned back onto the bed. He embraced himself. His cock jutting up towards the ceiling, throbbing. There appeared to be a mist or fog surrounding the large man lying next to me. He was, no doubt, in complete ecstasy.

"Yes, my little one, my boy. Daddy loves you too!" he kept repeating. David finally turned to look at me and held out his hand for me.

"Come, Nick! It's ok. He welcomes you. Come join us. Come closer!" David was looking at me, but not at me. It was like he was in a trance. I was feeling very awkward and somehow ashamed at seeing David's private moment. But I got up into a sitting position and David got on to his side, facing me. He put his hand on my chest.

"Joshua wants you to join us."

"What do you mean? Join us," I asked a little alarmed.

"Don't be frightened. This won't hurt. Trust us. Just lie back and relax. Now close your eyes." As I did so, the mist surrounded us both.

Incredible sensations came over me. Flashes of color came to my eyes, images of David and the boy. Oh, my God, I hadn't felt like that since my overindulgent drug days. Was I having a flashback? All my feelings were concentrated in my crotch. My cock felt bloated and huge. I was on top of David, in a reversed position, so his incredibly thick cock was in my face. I opened my mouth and stuffed as much of it into my mouth as I could. I felt David mimicking my movements. For one who hadn't had too much experience, he was doing a great job. We hungrily swallowed each other. Everything was happening so fast.

One moment we were in a 69 position, next I was on my hands and knees. David was leaning against the headboard, arms back. His thick legs were opened wide. I continued to suck his cock, at the same time someone was fucking me. I hadn't been in this position too many times in my life. I loved it. All the while a storm raged outside. The thunder was deafening and the lightning blinding. I couldn't remember the storm beginning. We sucked and fucked all the while as the storm built to an explosive crescendo. We shot together, moaning and gasping loudly. Our faces and chests soaked. As the storm ebbed and our orgasms subsided, we fell asleep in each others' arms, exhausted.

1st, November, Feast of All Saints

I woke up, as if from a drugged sleep. David was gone and in the air, hung the scent of chrysanthemums. On the pillow beside me was a single white mum. I picked it up and brought it to my nose. The smell brought back last night, David, the storm, the ghost, and the sex.

"Shit!" I said to myself. "What a night." I wondered how often David did this. I guessed he had more stamina than he showed last night.

In the cold reality of the morning light, I still doubted what happened. As I sit here at the kitchen table, with the morning sun filtering from the window. I tend to doubt what happened. Could it have been a shared dream, or had David giving me a drug and it was all a hallucination? The flower was no proof. Mums are common in fall. I have no real evidence.

Later - That week...

The week has gone by so fast. I am in a much better frame of mind. David has been here every day. Not that I mind. I wish I could take him home with me. Steal him away. Those eyes! I could easily get lost in them. But his place is here. This place, I lose myself in its ageless simplicity. In this place I find peace. But reality beckons, him to his world and me to mine. Sometimes he sleeps with me. I don't know what he tells his wife, I don't ask.

When this all started, I felt pity for the boy. I don't feel that way now. Watching David and hearing him talk to the boy; anyone would think he was crazy. But I've realized, the boy is not alone, he has David. He's found the father he's been searching for and the love. As for David, I don't know if it's healthy or not. But he's happy. He'll live out his life here. And in the end, they will be together, forever.

I'm just happy I was able to be a small part of their lives. I will come again and hopefully, be able to join with them again. If I don't, I will never forget, not David, not this place, and certainly not the ghost of Dark Oak Cottage.

~

About the Author

Nicolas Mann lives in a quiet neighborhood of Indianapolis, Indiana. There along with his partner Matthew, a dog named Gus and a cat named Lila, they live modestly and comfortably. He grew up in Northern Ohio, where as a child and teen, he ran along the shores of Lake Erie. In the spring of 1974 he moved to Chicago, where he spent most of his adult life. He studied art at The Academy of Art, and later applied to Columbia College to study writing but holds no degree.

He calls himself a dreamer and admits that his dreaming life is richer then his waking one. To him, dreams are like stories and stories are like dreams, they walk hand in hand in the realm of sleep. He began writing and drawing at an early age, but wasn't published until the early part of 1993 when, prompted by a friend, he submitted a story to Handjobs magazine. Since then he has worked with the HJ staff for several years, writing and drawing, and continues to this day. His stories have also appeared in other publications such as 100% Beef. Through the years his artwork has also graced the cover of Gay Chicago, Chicago's gay weekly magazine, and has appeared in ads for several bars.

You can contact him: mann.nicolas@gmail.com

~